CW00486321

AWAKENED LEADERS

HOW TO BECOME THE LEADER THE WORLD NEEDS NOW

BERYL PREUSCHMANN   ELAINE TROUP

GAIL PARTRIDGE   JENNIFER LEMON   DR JOY HESS

DR LIBBY MCGUGAN   MELANIE PECK

REBECCA HAMILTON   ROBIN MILES

Curated by
MEL MACINTYRE

INSPIRED WORLD PUBLISHING

Copyright © 2024

All rights reserved.

No part of this book may be reproduced in any form or by any electronic or
mechanical means, including information storage and retrieval systems, without
written permission from the author, except for the use of brief quotations in a book
review.

INTRODUCTION

A NEW WAY OF DOING BUSINESS FOR A NEW WORLD

My story

Once upon a time, I was a 'successful leader'. Working in a reputable organisation in an 'important' strategic role. Going through the motions each day to live my life, lead my team and try oh so hard to make a meaningful contribution.

But, I was also utterly lost. I walked through life with a continual yearning sensation that ebbed and flowed from a whisper to a scream...

'What's wrong with me? Why isn't this enough?'

Always faithfully accompanied by the shrill mean bitch who lives in the attic saying:

'Why can't you just be happy with what you have?

'You are so ungrateful to want more'

'What will other people think?

'You have a better life than so many.'

And then, something magical happened. I woke up one morning and had a breakdown.

I know it might not seem like the plot twist you were expecting (that came later!), but the wonderful thing about that morning is it was the day I decided to commit fully to my second bloom.

Who knew? That when I walked away from the career, home, friendship circle and city that I had worked so hard to call my own and threw my petals to the wind, that's what I was doing. I didn't.

There were few role models who felt relatable to me who had jumped off the cliff from a corporate career into the abyss of 'What else can I do?'

So I took the plunge and committed to working out how I could thrive professionally whilst also feeling authentic and aligned with my values, ethics and integrity.

I decided to set up my own business and leap into the world of entrepreneurship.

And I soon learned that I was not alone.

There were others out there who also felt like there had to be another way to live life and do business.

A way filled with more meaning. More fulfilment. More joy.

More freedom to dance to the beat of your own drum.

In fact, I began to connect with more and more people who were also searching.

Dissatisfied. Hungry for change. Thirsty for a deeper contribution.

These people became my tribe. My oxygen. My community. My clients. My friends.

And it fills my heart with so much joy to share some of their stories with you here in this magical, powerful book filled with tales of trauma, authenticity and the path of love in its many shapes and forms.

Why this, why now?

When we look at the world, it's become crystal clear to many of us who lead:

This. Isn't. It.

We can see our societal structures are not fit for purpose. They are founded on old, outdated ideas and fuelled by a toxic narrative that equates success with sacrifice.

Business with burnout.

And I believe many of us are awakening to this new perspective.

We are being called to step up and step forward to lead and succeed in a new way.

And, at the heart of the new model of success that is unfolding lives something as simple, eternal and ancient as time itself.

Love.

So in this book each author is sharing something very special with you.

Their story.

Each author has pulled back the curtain to share their journey, what they have learned along the way and the wisdom they want to impart.

What a special, sacred gift it is to share our pain and experiences with others, in the faith that they might triumph through their own trauma.

And each of us do that because we all believe *you and we* are important role models to lead the radical change required.

We believe with every ounce of our being, that if this book has found its way into your hands, it's because you too are an awakening leader with a contribution you feel called to make.

That your own personal and professional journey has awakened something in you that calls you to make a bigger difference in the world.

And so we invite you too, to take a stand.

To claim the cause you would die on a hill for.

And take action before you feel 'ready'.

And by doing so, become the leader the world needs now.

A delectable smorgasbord of stories with a huge dollop of love

It is my absolute delight to introduce you to the contributing authors who share their stories with us. I know you will gain just as much joy and insight from reading them as I did.

Libby's chapter focuses on the inherent wisdom within us all. Always there, patiently waiting for us to get quiet enough to hear the whispers that will lead us to our true nature and a more profound way of living and leading in life.

Gail implores us and reminds us in her chapter everyone is equal and as a leader your job is giving others space to shine. In fact, all you really need is love.

Robin shares not only her powerful story as a woman of colour in the USA but also her deep, academic research and insights gathered with rigour and gusto on love as an essential leadership characteristic for the 21st century.

Mel describes her journey through the darkness to fully unleash her light on and in the world. A true example of metamorphosis from larvae to a beautiful butterfly stretching her damp and tender new wings for all to see her true colours.

Jennifer delights us with her indomitable lemon spirit and how as she has changed and evolved, navigating the moments of bitterness and pith has unleashed her drive and desire to live life and love freely.

Rebecca lays down her rally cry for equality and through a game of business bingo highlights the ongoing challenges faced by women in business.

Joy shares her story of invisible leadership and the influence you can exert through gentle and relentless love for yourself and those you feel called to serve.

Elaine in her chapter calls out the silence that so often accompanies suffering. And her desire for us to share our truth with others believing it always helps.

Beryl takes us on a wild ride through time and space and shares her hard earned life lessons. Proving it's never too late to claim the life you want.

Who is this for?

In case you missed the memo, we wrote this book for you.

You may be teetering on the brink of burnout. Continuing to push through day after day.

Constantly spinning plates and struggling to relax. Wondering how to stop the hamster wheel of life and get off.

We see you. We wrote this for you.

Perhaps you've got your work like balance down already and you've got so much energy you don't know what to do with it all.

Determination in spades.

Purpose led with a big mission to fulfil.

Hungry for more. Dissatisfied with the status quo. Ready to unleash your light on the world.

We see you. We wrote this for you.

Perhaps you just want to read some great stories. You want something to inspire you during your summer vacay or holiday. Something more than fiction. Something real and tangible that can light a fire in your belly to be the change you want to be in the world.

We see you. We wrote this for you.

And if you don't identify with any of the above, *we still see you. And this is still for you.*

We see you and we see your beauty, essence and potential

You are divine energy embodied.

A walking miracle of chance.

You are nature in all its unbridled power and possibility.

A perfectly unique and imperfect human.

A one time only creation in the history of humanity - past and future.

You are wildly authentic.

It's your true nature.

And the world has never needed you more.

The world is changing and it's up to us to step forward and lead the way.

To build the courage and conviction to share our voices and make our presence felt.

To build a new foundation for humanity through doing business in a different way.

To weave new values based on love, compassion, equality, freedom and balance.

To redress the economic imbalance that threatens our world and our children's future.

And by doing so, rebuild our world one tender love fuelled choice at a time.

It's time to let your light shine and lead the way for others.

~Mel MacIntyre

ABOUT THE AUTHOR
MEL MACINTYRE

Mel MacIntyre is a 2 x international bestselling author, keynote speaker, in-demand coach & business strategist, and the founder of The Feminine Edge Business Incubator and Academy.

With 25+ years of experience as a leader, coach, and business consultant in a wide range of global businesses, Her favourite thing is seeing a woman step fully into her power to create financial freedom doing the work they love. Her research-based signature framework The Feminine Edge is designed to help women create more balance, impact, and success without risking burnout or selling out. Because she deeply believes, we *can* have it all. We just need to know how.

An extroverted hermit, you can find her with the wind in her hair and the sand in her toes hanging out with her partner Charlie and son Maximilian on her favourite beach on Eriskay, the tiny Hebridean island she calls home.

Mel is also an Ambassador for Women's Enterprise in Scotland using her voice to represent and promote women and their businesses.

- You can find her at www.melmacintyre.com and connect with her on LinkedIn https://www.linkedin.com/in/melaniemacintyre/

1

THE WISE CHOICE

DR LIBBY MCGUGAN

"Come to the edge
We might fall.
Come to the edge.
It's too high!
Come to the edge.
And they came,
And he pushed,
And they flew."

— *CHRISTOPHER LOGUE*

The choice point

It was 2013. I was sitting on the floor of a flat on the first night of my new life, surrounded by unpacked boxes. I had bought myself a packet of microwaveable rice for dinner, before I remembered that I didn't have a microwave. Recently separated, having moved back to the city, and having handed in my notice from a privileged position as an emergency medicine consultant, I realised I was at a choice point.

Here I was, no job, no partner, no income, no prospects, in a new place where I knew barely anyone. I could see both roads stretch out in front of me, almost signposted, and narrated by two voices in my head. Fear spoke on behalf of the first road, which was dark. *How can you possibly make things work at this stage in your life? Do you really expect to build things up again from scratch?*

The other road was light, and Excitement spoke for it. *This is a blank slate. Let's see what magic unfolds here.*

As tempting as it was to follow Fear, I chose the light.

Stepping off the cliff into the abyss, I had no idea what lay ahead.

I had moved out of the field of medicine into the cold because I knew I was missing something. Science and medicine were always a passion for me, and yet something within me was still restless. Having seen several people make full recoveries from conditions medicine could not cure, I was curious about what they were doing that was different. I began learning from them and others like them who had found a way to thrive through challenges.

I had no real plan, just a sense of curiosity and I simply followed the breadcrumbs. Isn't it interesting how life rises up to meet you when you have the courage to step out? Serendipitously, within a couple of months I crossed paths with the Chief Medical Officer for Scotland at the time, the wonderful Sir Harry Burns. He recommended me for a TEDx Talk, where I had the opportunity to share what I was learning. Eight days before the talk, my mum suffered a stroke. I stayed in hospital with her for three days and nights and was with her when she passed away. As painful as it was, it was her time to let go. Five days after she died, I presented the TEDx talk to 600 people. I was raw and even more impassioned to live life to the full and to share what I was learning.

What I was learning was this: there *is* more... so much more to discover. And it will blow your mind.

Organically, I began working with leaders, sharing what I could see was a direct path to living in flow, in harmony with life. I saw it in those I learned from – health champions, elite athletes, people who had found inner peace; I saw it in people I worked with, and I saw it in my own life, as circumstances began to shape themselves for the better in ways I could not have imagined.

It was becoming clear to me that there is another way of being that is available to all of us who are courageous enough to question and curious enough to look in the right direction.

As one of my clients puts it, '*It has been life-changing for me. I initially wanted a bit of a nudge in terms of career confidence but ended up with a complete shift that has positively impacted my whole life. Since working with Libby some amazing opportunities have opened up for me. The work that we did has opened me up to embrace these opportunities with confidence and joy.*'

What sets Awakened Leaders apart?

Our choices change things. With each choice we make, we expand into a new version of ourselves. Our personal minds have evolved to help us achieve remarkable things, with advancements in technology and standards of living beyond anything that was imaginable a hundred years ago. But, as a society, we have become wedded to our intellect and we're finding it's no longer enough. Living from intellect alone leads to isolation, separation and limitation. We're limited by assumption, comparison, competition and fear of the differences between us.

What sets Awakened Leaders apart is this: they have evolved in their *awareness*. They have become aware that there is more available to us *beyond* our personal mindset. They are aware that it is not just thinking or strategy or goals that matter, that it goes far deeper than this, to the core of who we are. And it's a highly practical and wonderful way to live, described as 'being twice as efficient with half the effort.' Awakened Leaders know that it is our *state of being* that changes everything.

As another client says, "*Very rarely would I say something has been life transformational, but this work has been massively life-changing.*"

What are we awakening to?

We're evolving from an era of knowledge-based leadership into an era rooted in Wisdom. Wisdom is bigger than knowledge. It brings us *new thoughts* we've not experienced before. Wisdom is not dependent on how long you've lived or how many years of experience you've gained. Wisdom, with a capital 'W' is *opening up* to a deeper intelligence within you that is bigger than your intellect. Does this make you uncomfortable?

When I work with people, the answer is usually 'yes'. We've become so used to living in our heads that we forget that there's more to us. It's like living in the attic of a beautiful mansion and never going downstairs. But when you do, you discover a depth, power and grace within you that you could not have imagined.

How do we access wisdom?

The first thing is to realise, it's already present within you. But here's the catch - you can't *think* your way into Wisdom. It is a knowing / feeling state of being that you experience and live by, rather than simply think about. Over the years I've distilled a framework for Inner Success that helps point people to the Wisdom within them, using six pillars:

Framework for Inner Success

Beyond The Personal Mind	High-Quality Decision Making	Discover Your True Nature	True Connection	Live Your Blueprint	Be The Role Model
Freedom	Inner Power	Inner Peace	Better Relationships	Clarity of Purpose	Inspire Others

The work we do points you to a deeper understanding of yourself and who you really are – and it gives you the freedom to live and to lead as this. Gaining a deeper understanding of the human system and how to work with it helps you *enjoy being* the best version of yourself. In the busyness of business, we sometimes forget that we are here to enjoy life. Discovering who you really are, you'll find, will bring you both joy and Wisdom.

This understanding goes beyond psychology – it clarifies and simplifies why you are held back, disengaged or overwhelmed and helps you regain control in shaping your experience for the better. It brings you back to your place of inner power.

Naturally and automatically, you begin to lead from a *conscious state of being* rather than simply the strategy of the personal mind. This state of being has a powerful positive impact on people, their teams and society. Here, you feel more at peace within yourself, more authentically connected with others. Your value is evident and your performance more efficient with far less stress.

The key elements

There are four things I would love you to take from this:

1. The intelligence of Wisdom

Wisdom is what's present when we open up *beyond* what we think we know. Again, this often makes people uncomfortable. Our personal minds like to know everything. They don't *actually* know, they just like to think that they do. Have you ever had a problem you can't solve, and end up feeling completely frustrated? That's your personal mind believing that it should know and refusing to admit that it doesn't. The truth is, there is a bigger part of us that does know the answer: this is Wisdom.

The answers we're looking for lie in Wisdom. It's the space of *higher quality thinking and solutions, which is beyond our personal thinking.* And this is key for leaders to understand. Countless relationships – personal, professional and international – and billions of pounds are wasted each year because people make decisions from the wrong place; from personal assumptions rather than from Wisdom.

Wisdom is beyond our personal minds. When you open up and trust, you'll know what you need to know when you need to know it, and you can relax. No more holding onto tension about not knowing. *Simply knowing that there is an answer and that it will occur to you*, is enough. Can you see how liberating this is?

How much do you trust life? I mean, really trust life? Is making the sun come up on your to-do list? What about ensuring the right amount of gravity so that you don't fall up? And then there's that cut to heal, the hair to grow, those cells to regenerate...

When you really look at how much is taken care of *for us,* you begin to see that we don't have to work it all out. Take a look around - the intelligence of nature knows how to create things from seeds – including us. It wrote the operating manual on how to run things. It knows what it's doing. This intelligence inbuilt in the system is on our side and the odds are stacked in our favour. If they weren't, we would have died out eons ago.

If you've already decided that things are going to be difficult, then you've just closed the door on possibilities that would make things easier. Opening up to trusting life a little more each day gives life the space it needs to help you out, in highly practical ways that will surprise and delight you. This brings the magic of creation back into leadership. You don't always need to know the answers to lead, you just need to know where to look to find them. Can you feel how fresh and clear and new this makes things?

2. You are the artist and thought is your palate

"Thought creates our world and then says, 'I didn't do it.'"

— *DAVID BOHM*

Everything is thought, but it's so easy to miss this. Even the chair you're sitting on began as a thought in someone's mind. The computer or phone you're reading from began as thought in someone's mind and, with the help of other thoughts from other minds, became a reality.

But in the process, we lose sight of the origin of creation; the power of thought.

When you slow down and see this power and how it flows through you, you can begin to create from a new place.

As a leader, you're a creator. You're shaping the path for yourself, your team and your organisation, whether you're fully conscious of this or not.

One of the questions I usually ask clients is *'Where do you think your experience comes from?'*

It's amazing to me how this single question leads people to step back into their power. Not power over anyone else, but *empowerment;* power within themselves. It always surprises me how far this can take us in realising our ability to shape our experience for the better.

Take a moment and consider this for yourself. Does your experience come from other people? From how well your business is doing? The state of the market? Or something else? Grab a journal, set aside a few minutes for yourself, and write it down.

It's easy to think that our experience of life comes from things 'out there' that happen to us.

But when you look more closely, you begin to see that we're not dealing with situations or events or other people; we're dealing with *our thoughts about those things.* Events are neutral - it's our thoughts about them that give them meaning and make us *feel* the way we do.

This is bad news and good news...

The bad news is that we're responsible for our experience.

The good news is that we're responsible for our experience!

Initially it can be daunting to realise that we have this level of responsibility. But rather than it being a burden, it becomes a superpower when we see that *we have a choice* about where we place our attention. And what we give our attention to, comes to life.

We may not be able to change the thoughts that pass through our minds, but we do have the choice about how much attention we give them. The more attention we give to thoughts, the more life will reflect them back to us in our experience. Whenever you're feeling upset or annoyed about other people or events, try this...

Take a few deep breaths, let go of all thinking for a few moments and let your mind clear. Open up to the space within you beyond the noise of your thinking. Sooner or later, a fresh thought will arrive with a new perspective about things *that feels better*. This is the space of Wisdom. Notice that you don't have to try hard to figure it out. Accessing this deeper intelligence means that the solution *will occur to you*. It takes the effort and striving out of the equation and allows you to feel more ease and flow throughout your day.

3. Feelings are a tuning fork

As a society, we now find it easier to embrace feelings, but they are still widely misunderstood. Most people consider feelings as something to be analysed or fixed or tolerated or feared. We deal with them by sharing the stories behind them, by suppressing them or by worrying about what they mean. But Wise leaders understand the role of feelings – they give us our experience of life, moment to moment, and they *tell us whether the thoughts we're thinking are aligned with Wisdom, or not*.

When you really get this, you realise that feelings are indicators – like the light on your dashboard letting you know you need fuel – they are simply telling us whether we're aligned with the best perspective for us, or whether we're missing something. Nothing else. It's only when our personal minds jump in and make up a story or assumption around a feeling that things get complicated. Feelings in their truest sense are much simpler. They are friendly indicators – make friends with them, notice what they're pointing you to, or away from, and see what happens.

You can try this now. Focus on a recent experience that you enjoyed and notice how it feels. Was it a walk with the dog? Time with your partner or your children or your friends? Connection with your team? A great result for your business? The good feelings are telling you that those thoughts are on track and are helpful for you.

Now bring your attention to an experience that you didn't enjoy and notice how you feel. Was it tension in a meeting? Frustration over a deadline? Overwhelm of balancing family and work life? Notice the stories that creep up around those memories... what are they saying about you or others or the world? These uncomfortable feelings are telling you that you're missing something: there is another perspective available to you that is better for you. Like putting your hand on a hot stove is meant to hurt so that you pull your hand away and don't burn it, uncomfortable feelings are *meant to be uncomfortable* because they're trying to get you to shift your attention away from unhelpful stories. Without negative feelings, we would have no feedback, no way of knowing whether our focus is on track and aligned with Wisdom, or not. Feelings are here to help guide us.

4. The world is your mirror

Everything is energy. Does *this* make you uncomfortable? Some people still associate the word 'energy' with being a bit hippy-dippy. But if you look at the physics of things, you see that everything, at its most essential level, is energy in motion. We know that everything we can see in the Universe is made of matter. Matter is made of molecules, atoms and subatomic particles, which are made of vibrating energy. But did you know that all the matter we can see makes up for only 4% of what is actually here? There's more to the Universe than the matter we can see. 96% of it is formless energy... Which means 96% of you is formless energy.

We're living in a field of *intelligent* energy, exchanging information between everyone and everything. We're broadcasting and receiving energy every moment, mostly subliminally. The energy we broadcast leaves an imprint on the field which ripples out to impact everyone and everything... it physically changes the fabric of reality. You know this - have you ever walked into a room and sensed an atmosphere without anyone saying a word? Do you know someone who lights the place up as soon as they walk in? We're picking up information from all around us, constantly. We're also sending out energetic signals and life will reflect back to us circumstances and interactions that match that signal. The world is our mirror. Have you ever got out of the wrong side of the bed and found your whole day spiralling downhill? And ever decided to feel good and watched as life brought you new surprises and chance encounters?

Becoming conscious of what we're broadcasting is growing up. One of the areas I love most about working with Awakened Leaders is seeing them consciously choose to set the tone for themselves, their team and their company, because they know this will change what comes back to them.

Wise leaders know this and they *practise* this every day.

One leader I've been working with recently is fully embracing living from Wisdom. Even in the face of significant challenges in his organisation, with some very difficult decisions to be made, he focused on setting the tone with his team as the priority before anything else. Excellence and Trust are now the agenda, rather than strategy. Moving from Wisdom, rather than micromanaging, he trusts his team fully to deliver their best, and gives them space to do so. And they have delivered far beyond any expectations. Not only that, they now lead *their* teams from Wisdom, giving them the space to step up and contribute in their best ways. This Wise leader has started his own powerful positive ripple effect. He knows now that strategy limits us to what we define as achievable, whereas Wisdom frees us to rise beyond this, and realise our potential in ways we have yet to discover.

The big choice point

I love working with changemakers. Leaders who have a vision of how they can contribute to making the world a better place, not just for themselves, but for their families, their team, their organisations and our wider society.

Whatever their role is, they are more than that. They recognise that they are part of something bigger and that they matter in showing up for this.

We are at a choice point in our evolution as a society. We can choose to continue down the path of Fear – separation, conflict and suspicion - or we can choose the path of Wisdom – collaboration, trust and freedom.

All of the conflicts of the world – whether in relationships at home or between countries – are due to people innocently making decisions and taking action from fear-based thinking and assumptions.

We have a real opportunity to turn things around. The more of us who wake up to Wisdom, the more chance we have of changing the trajectory of humanity to one that our children will be proud of.

Leaders are in a prime position to lead by example and to reset the trajectory. If you want to see change 'out there' it has to start 'in here', within you. Will you be part of it?

"*You are not just a drop in the ocean.*
You are the mighty ocean in the drop."

— *RUMI*

ABOUT THE AUTHOR
DR LIBBY MCGUGAN

Dr Libby Mcgugan is an executive coach, TEDx speaker and published author. She works with forward-thinking leaders who want inner success - the freedom, empowerment and peace of mind to live and lead as their true selves - for a balanced, fulfilling life. She loves this work as it shifts people from fear to wisdom and opens them up to make powerful positive changes in themselves, their organisation and the world.

Her background as a medical doctor gives leaders a simple and clear approach to a much deeper understanding of the human system and how to work with it to achieve success from the inside out.

She is the published author of three books: *The Eidolon,* for which she was nominated Best Newcomer in the British Fantasy Awards, its sequel, *The Fifth Force* and her non-fiction book, *The Power of the Lemon.* She lives in Scotland with her partner, Graham and loves playing the fiddle in his band, Bensider.

- You can find her on her website: libbymcgugan.me
- Join her email list and download her Inner Success Framework here: https://www.libbymcgugan.me/inner-success-framework
- Find her on LinkedIn as Dr Libby McGugan: https://www.linkedin.com/in/dr-libby-mcgugan-153979180/

2

ALL YOU NEED IS LOVE

GAIL PARTRIDGE

Why is it that people would follow you to the end of the earth? A colleague once asked me this and I didn't really know how to answer the question. What I did know, was I loved what I was doing, and I loved my team, I loved every single one of them. Yes, there were some that performed better and more consistently than others, but because I loved them, I was more curious than frustrated.

In one of my first roles, after leaving school, I worked for someone who brought in fancy biscuits every time his boss was coming to visit from down south. I remember thinking, at the time, why would you do that? It was an attempt to impress him. One thing I knew for sure was that I never wanted anyone to feel they had to behave in a different way or 'buy fancy biscuits' to impress me. The term 'buy me fancy biscuits' is one I use in coaching or leadership when I think that someone is trying to impress me or saying what they think I want to hear.

Oh, and no one person deserves fancy biscuits over another. I still remember that little bit of feeling valued disintegrated that day. I also believe it shaped the leader I became – everyone is equal, and everyone deserves love and nurture.

Feeling valued has been a big thing for me all my life. Growing up, and still now, my parents tell me how proud they are of me. Even when it was hard to watch me moving away from home, they supported me, they believed that I could fly.

The centre of all of it is love and giving others space to shine.

Just a wee girl from Glasgow

I was 27 and in my first big job in London – me a wee girl from Glasgow, a Global Customer Service Manager.

It was at a time when customer experience was at the heart of everything my team and I were trying to do. I had a leader who believed in me and valued the work I did and the way I led my team.

We were a global team who had service centres dotted across the world. Our European service centres were outsourced to a third party and our customers were not getting the service and experience they deserved in one of the regions.

We had to part company with our outsource partners. Leading with my gut, I felt the best thing we could do was bring the service back in-house to service our customers with our own people.

We were faced with opening a centralised service centre in London, with different systems and technology, speaking eight different languages. *In six weeks.*

I told our Executive Team that my team could do this. We had a space for the team to sit but everything else had to be sourced, the people, the languages, the technology, the hardware, the telephony - the list goes on. I had the right people; I knew that, and I handed all of the deliverables over to them.

I trusted they could do it and my message to them was: "Do what needs to be done and let me know what I have to do to clear the path for you". The team included one person who would be running the operation and his role was to set up and resource it. I had another who was excellent with IT and had some brilliant relationships in that area. I had someone who was winding down the relationship with the third party and was working to bring anyone that wanted to come over to work in the centre. I had a project manager.

My role, to clear the path for them to do great work. That was all I did. I loved and respected each one of them and I knew in my heart that they would do this. I managed the stakeholders and kept any pain that came with the project away from them. I was there to coach them and help them remove any barriers or self-doubt. Six weeks later, we opened our new centre with eight languages and all the connectivity it required.

And oh, how we celebrated.

Everything was going great guns for me, I left that organisation with a great legacy and then went into a large, fast-paced media organisation. There was a bit of a 'boys club' with men using nicknames for each other, which made the women in the organisation feel a bit left out, or like they had to behave like them to succeed. Which was never my thing. It was still exciting.

During this time, I married Paul, and we were gifted with our beautiful daughter Zoe, who will always be my greatest achievement.

Along with that came, postnatal depression. The shock of what was happening to me was so overwhelming. I had been this young, successful businesswoman and all of a sudden, I couldn't lift my head off the pillow. I had travelled all over the world on my own for work but I found I couldn't be alone. Every day, when Paul went to work, I would go into the car and drive straight to my mum's where I would cry all day and feel I couldn't be trusted to be Zoe's mum. My beautiful daughter, all I had ever dreamed of, and I wasn't strong enough to be her mum.

It was a horrific, very vulnerable time for me. I was this uber confident career woman, who had all the trappings, beautiful house, wonderful husband, beautiful baby girl and great family and friends and I didn't feel I could ever be happy again.

Of course, it passed. Not without the help of The Priory and antidepressants, but it passed.

I never say I suffered from mental illness but what truly happened was I learned who I really was and what I was capable of. I understand vulnerability and how it feels to be so low that you think there is no light. It taught me a lot, about myself, but it also taught me empathy. I remember being asked how I could be depressed when I had everything most people would ever want. I know how it feels to have everything but feel nothing. I use what I learned through this time in my life to understand that all you really need is love. It starts with self-love.

I had to learn to love myself again. And I did. I brought myself back to that fun loving, outgoing strong woman. I am also the best mum that Zoe could ever have, and I will never let anyone say otherwise.

I also knew I could never be a stay-at-home mum. Just didn't have it in me. I came into this world to make a difference and we decided that our daughter would grow up surrounded by others and be a strong woman in her own right.

I wanted to be a role model for her, that she could be whatever she wanted.

So back to work I went, and it was all going really well until it wasn't.

I had moved industries when Zoe was around five years old. I was in a role which was definitely not utilising me to my full potential, but, in a way, it suited me as Zoe was still young and Paul and I were both juggling childcare and school runs.

After a couple of years in that role, my manager left due to burn out. I was a bit of a square peg in a round hole in this role, but it was fine. Although I could see where I could really make a difference I was never really allowed to do so.

When the new manager started, things started to go downhill. I was always a good or excellent performer, so, content in my role.

The first time I met him, the first thing he said to me was 'I hear people think you are pretty good at what you do. Well, I don't know you from Adam and you will have to prove yourself before I think you are any good'.

When he handed me my bonus letter, he told me to make the most of it as, from what he had seen, it wouldn't be happening again.

He told me that one of the Directors had asked to see him to talk about my poor performance. This was not true as I asked the Director what was wrong, and he didn't know what I as talking about

The list goes on. The little voice in my brain: 'You're not good enough, you knew that one day you would be found out.' I think they call it gaslighting now but to me it was bullying.

My mental health took a tumble, and I was back to feeling useless and helpless again. I was crying on every train journey home at night, not sleeping, scared to go to work in the morning.

I had no choice but to leave.

I was never going to let that happen to me again.

I was going to make it my life's work to make sure that others didn't go through what I did. If I can stop one person being bullied, gaslit, whatever you want to call it, I would.

I spent the next few months with lots of leaders understanding how they operated and how they were received by their team. Different styles and different ways of working emerged.

I then reflected on the question I posed at the beginning of this chapter and thought about why would anyone be led by me?

I realised that what I was doing was creating the space for them to do their best work. I never tried to command and control them; I was there to serve them.

As a leader, command and control = compliance and status quo. Being of service to your team results in commitment and innovation.

Having a desire to serve your team means that you care so much about them succeeding, that you are willing to do whatever it takes to enable and empower them to succeed.

Be happy to stand aside and let them take the glory.

My leadership journey has been an emotional one in many ways. I know how it felt to be led when someone really valued me and also to be led by someone who, without doubt, wanted to make me feel worthless. You can probably guess which one enabled and empowered me and which one saw me as competition, even though they were my boss!

You see, it all starts with how you show up. What is the mindset you are choosing? That is the crux of it – you can choose your mindset. You can choose how you react to certain circumstances – you had a bad morning; you can choose to put that in a box. What are people's first impressions of you at any given time? What is it like to be on the other side of you? I once met a leader who was proud to be known as a Rottweiler with lipstick, not a look I would recommend.

Here is the trick, I call this 'The tonight Matthew moment' which comes from and old TV show, where people came on to the show as an ordinary everyday person then as they walked through a set of sliding doors they would say 'Tonight Matthew, I am going to be Tina Turner' or any other star.

You choose your own version of the 'sliding door'. For me it is walking through my office door in the morning, or stepping out of my car when I am out and about. I choose my mindset and how people will experience me.

Tonight Matthew...I am going to be curious and present.

What is happening here is that I am tapping into my Emotional Capital. I was so excited to find out that this was a thing. So, when I think about the question that I was asked about why people would follow me, it is down to how I use my Emotional Capital to guide me in my leadership.

I became an Awakened Leader.

I once read a book called Head, Heart, and Guts by Dotlich, et al. It was a bit of a lightbulb moment for me in that it explained who I am as a leader. Leading with the Head only, shows up as the person who is trying to be the cleverest in the room. Leading from the Heart is leading with your emotions and feelings which in isolation can make a person not want to rock the boat for fear of upsetting anyone and leading with guts in isolation may be a bit over risky. After reading this I realised that the blend I was using wasn't wrong. I was just surrounded with so many people who were leading with their heads and trying to be the cleverest person in the room.

As leaders we need to know enough to have credibility, but not always be the expert in everything as that's why we hire great people. We need to love enough, to ensure we lead in service of those in our teams to feel empowered and psychologically safe. And be brave enough to go with our gut at the times when we know intuitively it is the right thing to do.

The centre of all of it is love and emotion. The head part we can learn and the guts part comes from trust and intuition and that comes from how emotionally connected you feel with your own intuition and self-belief and your trust and belief in others.

I believe, and there is research that backs this belief, that leading people towards success and their optimum performance is all down to emotion. As I said before, the desire to serve and clear the path of any obstacles, does not require you to be the cleverest person in the room (although some IQ is useful), it requires you to understand the capabilities of others and have the feeling in your heart and guts, that you know and trust that people have a full rucksack of potential on their back to be the best they can be.

And the research... Daniel Goleman concluded through research carried out on the power of Emotional Intelligence, that 90% of a leader's success is down to Emotional Quotient (EQ) and 10% down to IQ.

I knew I had to do something to support leaders to bring out the best in themselves and their people and business.

I had dived deep into the world of Emotional Capital (EQ) following the work of Martyn Newman. He identified that there are 10 competences that underpin EQ e.g., Self-Awareness, Self-Reliance. So, I got myself a licence to use the Emotional Capital profiling tool and designed a framework to work with leaders on how they can be their authentic self with skill.

I always say, 'I am just a wee girl from Glasgow'. Where that used to be my imposter, it has now become my superpower. Being this straight-talking Glaswegian who is bursting with love, is why my clients want to work with me.

Too much time is wasted trying to fit a mould. The key to success is being your UNIQUE self and knowing how to bring that every day.

Being UNIQUE is down to the following:

Unleash who you really are and make that work for you. Think about when am I at my best - What am I doing? How am I being? What results am I getting? How am I feeling? How am I showing up for others?

Navigate and Nurture relationships. Spend time with others, find out what matters to them and how you can help them succeed. Be upfront about what you need from them to be at your best. Make time to nurture and support others and them you.

Identify the things that knock you off track. Once you know them you can be accountable for them and choose whether they are in your control or influence or whether you have to Shut Up and Move On. You can never change other people, but you can understand them and support them.

Quick fixes. Identify the things you can just do to help yourself and others to perform. Clear the path for others. You have nurtured your relationships; people will clear the path for you.

Understand that there are times when you need to adapt your style as you may not be everyone's cup of tea. This is called being yourself with skill.

And finally, be:

Everything you are, with all that you have.

When I work with clients through this model, we start to uncover the real person that they are and what they are capable of just by more self-love and understanding of others. We talk about how they may need to adapt to others in a way that they can still be authentic. It takes courage to use emotion and not just fit the mould. In doing this work you won't need to buy fancy biscuits to impress others (remember that from the beginning of this chapter) you will ooze personality and humility.

All you need is to understand, embrace and love your UNIQUE self, then you show up with love and compassion and developed Emotional Capital. You will see.

All you need is love.

ABOUT THE AUTHOR
GAIL PARTRIDGE

Gail Partridge is a Business Performance Coach and Leadership Expert with PGZ Consulting Ltd. She helps busy leaders who are struggling with the many complex relationships in today' s business environment. She does this by tapping into the emotional side of leadership that helps to realise the potential of their UNIQUE authenticity to drive optimum performance. She does this through using straightforward, straight-talking leadership and coaching programmes and stays right by your side until you don't need her anymore.

She is an ICF accredited coach, Insights Behavioural Assessor and Emotional Capital Accredited Coach.

Gail lives in Stirling in Scotland with her husband, Paul, daughter Zoe and of course Darcy Dog.

She is always singing and is part of a Rock Choir in her spare time.

She has a deep-rooted belief that love is always the answer.

- You can find her on www.pgzconsulting.co.uk and https://www.linkedin.com/in/gail-partridge-6b59795/.

3

CHOOSE LOVE? CRY OUT FOR 'LOVE LEADERSHIP'

CREATE CONTINUOUS GROWTH AND CREATIVE FLOW

REBECCA HAMILTON

Something has to change in the way that we all work and live. My realisation came in skips and jolts. But I know now - there is a better way, there is a different way.

Here's a story. I'm on all fours, on the floor of a meeting room, gasping for breath. I've always been good in a crisis and this was no different. My brain went to the filing cabinet, found the checklist titled 'heart attack' and starting skimming through to assess the situation. I heard myself saying 'I can't breathe, give me a minute', factual and directive. Meanwhile, water was pouring down my face, while my intel gauged 'not normal crying'. After my breath had come back to my body, I went into what I thought was physical shock. I now know it was an adrenaline hangover – and I went to sleep for 14 hours.

Your body will always find a way to bring you back to the truth of a moment, a space, a relationship, an environment or a workplace that does not serve you. In hindsight, you'll realise that you already knew. Your instinct had forewarned you some time ago. Your intuition said 'this isn't right' - coupled with gut wrenches, stomach flips, confused gaps and tears of pure frustration.

Of course, this spontaneous, involuntary cat cow was not the first time my body dramatically told me 'enough'.

When I found out about my husband's first affair, I collapsed. Then, four people in my family died in relatively quick succession. A cloud of sadness, coupled with uplifting gratitude, became the post-traumatic-growth-life-rhythm. And then I found out my husband was having a baby with another woman. My legs stopped working so my wretch of a husband had no choice but to hold my body upright as it retched into the toilet bowl, hour after hour.

These signs are sirens saying stop. Klaxon horns - "something is wrong".

We find ourselves in professional and personal environments that are broken. That are simply not working. Our intuition may warn us – but our body will say 'listen'.

Look, my personal view these days is that post-traumatic growth is awesome. Yes, I did just say that. I may even have got addicted to the growth so much that the effect it created became my new way of living *forever*. Seriously. Transforming trauma so that adversity becomes advantage is a neural pathway *win*. Trust me. *The secret is to take the way of life that becomes natural in post-traumatic growth - and live like that, all the time.* Continuous growth and creative flow is how I roll now.

Long, long ago, as a very young child, I grasped the power of peacemaking and creating harmony in my environment; some would say our family went through trauma at that time. It developed me as an empath and as such gave me acute intuition.

Then, when I was a teenager, I made adverts at lunchtime to help people decide what they wanted to eat from the school canteen.

Later, I got into marketing as a career choice because I believed in it for the power of good: to understand individuals and connect in a way that would touch their heart and make the world a happier place.

I got into business because of Anita Roddick. She made me believe there is a different way and – we can change the world. Business as unusual, she said. Sign me up, I said.

I've been working in business for more than 25 years. I'm an intuitive leader. I *feel* decisions, solutions and strategy. I've worked with some of the greatest leaders and mentors, learning what fair, intelligent, compassionate, collaborative and creative leadership looks like. With groups of wonderful people working together, we've delivered wonderful pieces of work. I have worked with great men and women all my career. I am grateful for the good people – and even the not so good ones. I marry art and science; and I'm a creator and an aspiring athlete. I blend my approach.

I have watched, seen, thought, felt, sensed and marched my way through my working life, constantly developing. I have a high EQ, a strong sense of self awareness and I am blessed with a chipper and positive mindset. I take huge bites out of life with a grateful grin on my face and joy in my heart.

I am generally beside myself to be here.

When that's not the case – I do the work to reset to a growth mindset. This is how I choose to be.

This is why I know that *parts* of how we work and live are broken.

I'm calling it out. We can do better and we can change the world for the better and live greater lives.

Do you ever look around you and whisper quietly, 'what the fuck?', as you gaze with wonder, bemused and agog, at what is occurring. I know I'm not alone (sometimes I hear you, and try not to snort out loud.)

So, traditional corporate business and 'the way the world is designed' is largely alpha culture. It just is. It's partly why there aren't enough toilets when I go to the rugby – and why there aren't pockets on my skinny jeans to stash my hip flask.

Once upon a time, there was a white man called Walter... etc, etc, etc. The majority of the world was designed specifically for a minority 'type' of the world. Beyond gender, this creates a weighting of characteristics, style, traits, decisions, that don't really work for everyone and don't get the best results.

This is a problem because it means the world is out of balance, most of the time. And it means I can't share a sip of whisky at the game on a cold January day.

In a workplace and business environment, imbalance shows up, souring culture and slowing down performance.

Profit without care for purpose or people, with no real sight on long-term legacy. Ego-led environments resulting in unhealthy or toxic competition, aggressive, one-upmanship and defensiveness. Bias and discrimination silencing suggestions that will make a difference and make people feel that they have a voice. Misguided belief that working hard makes for success as humans hurtle towards burn out.

These traits are stealthy when they turn up. Meetings take four times longer than needed as statements are made - one after another, round and round the table, like dogs barking, without listening and building to a quick and collaborative outcome. A canny suggestion is made and falls on deaf ears – then *someone else* says it, to praise and applause? Nitpicking sceptics kill a potentially brilliant business move at birth. These inefficient and ineffective subtleties suck joy and energy out of the room and – the world. They stop our continuous growth and creative flow.

Is there simply a lack of love*?

"What the world needs now, is love, sweet love"

— HAL DAVID

Dear reader, let's plaaaaaaaay... **Cry Out Bingo!**
• What on earth is going on?
• What are we doing?
• Why is it like this?
• This is a waste of time!
• This is sucking the life out of me!
• We can do better!
• Just, no! Time is running out, folks, pay attention.

From my own perspective – as a senior professional female, white woman, working in corporate business, my perspective is half-lifetime so far.

This is not about man v woman – it's not that crude.

As an empath female, brought up by two male feminists (plus strong women and a village that measures success on how you show up in the community), I'm often shocked or bemused at how business - and our wider society - behaves.

I have been a solo woman in a room with four (or 14) men on countless occasions. Yes, it requires disproportionately harder work than if the numbers were switched. The impact of bias (conscious or otherwise) is undeniable.

Yes, you'll recognise it. Picture the scene with me...

I'm about to be the main act in a presentation on strategy – I'm standing, sipping a coffee. A man clad in tweed blusters in, looks me up and down, and commands "white with one".

I'm 24 years old, sitting at a table with 15 white, middle-aged men. We are all there as 'equal representatives'. Every time I speak – there is a cough and I am ignored.

I'm the only woman in the room – verbally giving my view. Mid sentence, a hand goes up towards my face, in parallel to a 'sssshhhhhh', as I am silenced mid flow.

I take a call from a senior male – he wants to 'borrow' a female from my team. I offer a male alternative for the task. The request suddenly disappears.

I've just been made a Fellow of The Chartered Institute of Marketing. I walk into the House of Lords. I am met with a long look down my 6 foot of evening gown and a, "What are you doing here?". I am a Fellow, chaps, like you, I reply.

Come on. It's visible, a waste of time, sucks the soul out of life. And it's soooo boring.

But more importantly – it's a drag factor to higher performance and success. This is the critical point.

This is the clear double conundrum – and part of the answer as to why it could be different.

Women are not taken as seriously as men – that is a fact. As Mary Ann Sieghart writes in 'The Authority Gap', "bias may be unconscious but it nonetheless leads them to undervalue and disrespect female colleagues. They may not notice they are doing it, but the women at the receiving end certainly do. And unconscious bias is harder to call out, as the perpetrator – affronted – is likely to deny its very existence."

And, "Men behave worse when they outnumber women. Put a woman in a meeting with four men, and 70% of the interruptions she receives from men are negative. Turn it around so you have four women and one man: just 20% of the interruptions women receive from men are negative. When women predominate, 'Men undergo a drastic change. They become far less aggressive'."

Swimming up river, against the current, while our male counterparts unconsciously cruise on the tide, is frustrating, to put it mildly.

But our second side of the conundrum penny – beyond 'simply' (ho, ho, ho) not being taken seriously - is that feminine (not necessarily female) leadership traits hold hints as to how we could achieve a better world with better business and happier humans (and a happier planet, I would wager).

The evidence is abundant.

Twenty-five Fortune 500 companies with the best record of promoting women into high positions were 18% to 69% more profitable.

Women outscored men on 17 of the 19 capabilities that differentiate excellent leaders.

Having women in the c-suite is associated with higher profitability.

Women surpass men in 11 of 12 major emotional intelligence characteristics – including emotional self-awareness, flexibility and teamwork. And valuable personalities include good communicators, Empaths and self-aware individuals who are conscious of their strengths and weaknesses.

Yet, all around the world, 'DE&I initiatives', 'Women Leader Initiatives' and 'Plans For Female Entrepreneurs' - while all necessary and much welcomed – are chipping away at the hard edges of an established machine, designed by that chap-Walter-wot-the-world-was-designed-for and his chums some time ago. Lean in? Sod that. Step back.

So, if a different leadership style is outperforming in the established 'way' – what could we do if we *all* adopted an alternative – if we weren't all pushing against the old, shiny, Walter approved machine?   Could we redesign the way we work and live to swim in flow together?

Imagine how far and how fast we would go.

Schools would be nurture first, business better and more profitable – people and purpose built in, the world more peaceful and we - as a human race living a shared planet with nature and the creatures of earth - would be happier. We all need purpose beyond ourselves.

Sounds big right? Surely the easy bit is a shift in how we work.

The anti-mushy brigade will hate this – but I believe in the power of love to change business. To live and work in a state of continuous growth and creative flow coming from a place of love. I choose to choose love.

My view is there is no alternative – unless we want a poorer result for ourselves and everyone else. A colleague once asked if it was disruptive to use the word 'love'. If it is, I say – good, here's to healthy disruption.

LovE Leadership: continuous growth and creative flow.

LovE with a capital E: with 7 ways to lovE.

Let's go.

1. Equality

I sat in a 'Women's Workshop' in 2018 and heard 'it will be over 100 years to reach equality for pay'. 'We'll all be dead!', we cried. In 2019, the WEF, told us it would be 99 years to reach equal footing as men in political influence, economic gain and health and education. Five years on, I'm a glass half full sort of person – but I'll still be dead.

Look, we're not 'the same'. We are different in so many ways, which is to be celebrated. We may show up and apply ourselves differently – but we all do want equal opportunity and reward.

94 years is too far away.

Apparently we have 'gender fatigue'. But, research* suggests some strategically ignore gender inequality: when presented with incidents of discrimination they would say it had nothing to do with gender.

Leadership *must* place real equality at the heart of how we all behave.

Live for Equality: Learn how to spot it. As in – properly. If you don't know what it looks or feels like – do the work. If you know what it feels like but you don't know how to call it out – talk about the facts, how it happens, how it makes you feel. Lead a conversation – make noise. Make bold decisions and take action. Raise a table tennis bat like an air traffic controller every time it happens – do something.

Cry Out Bingo: "Give me a break – I don't have 94 years!"

2. 0-Ego

Of course. Ego unchecked and not understood – can fight off intuition to a point where it may damage your soul.

Ego can be destructive – showing up as self-centeredness, superiority or a lack of compassion. It can harm decision making – and displays as arrogance and entitlement. Yes, it is also sensitive to judgement, criticism and failure. Coming from a place of fear, the bigger the ego – the bigger resistance you will feel when you try to suggest change or a new idea.

I'm an intuitive leader – I feel decisions and answers. I trust my gut – and I know when I am working in 80% intuition and 20% ego that I am doing my best work. Some people who operate from 80% ego and rely on thinking their way through decisions – can struggle with an intuitive style. You burn way more energy trying to 'think it' out. My intuition is sound – uses less energy and is swift, quick and accurate.

Live for 0-Ego: Do the work to feel, understand and interpret what is unconscious and deep in your intuition. Aim for close to zero ego. Only allow your ego one *passenger* seat in the spacious SUV and *balance* that motherfucker's point of view.

Cry Out Bingo: "I know the answer – trust me!"

3. Energy

We are all just a manifestation of energy, in mass particle form – at a moment in time. Blogs and pages talk about leaders 'managing their energy' - logically, physically. Some refer to 'relational' energy.

A woman's cycle is 28 days long – and a man's is only 24 hours. That's 28 hormone cycles in the time a woman goes through one – as does a lunar cycle of the moon (and that's no coincidence). Consider what this means for energy flow – and then add all the other affecting factors.

We can 'feel bad energy' in a room - or be 'low on energy' after a caffeine slump. We can affect our own energy cycle; or someone else's - and we absorb other people's energy.

There is no prescription or 'formula' - we are all different. Energy is felt, experienced, understood and balanced uniquely to you. Rigid approaches at work might not suit the majority. Maximising energy is the name of the game.

When I talk about my Energy it is with a big E – my own energy within myself; the space and people I spend time with and the wider and higher energy of life ('The Universe', if you like).

I work to understand, balance and maximise mine: how it gives and takes. I do things to soothe, protect and strengthen physically, mentally and spiritually to be in creative flow and align to my soul.

Highly nutritious, mostly mediterranean diet. Sleep discipline. Morning ritual. Balancing yin and yang fitness regime. I practise grounding. I chat to the odd tree or bumble bee. I meditate, go inward (dude). I seek out high energy and creative flow environments. I spend time with people that feed my soul – and run away from people that do not.

Live for Energy: Own and know your energy and its flow, in and out. Stay in creative flow. Do whatever it takes – for you. Be ready to recover and run. And stay soul aligned.

Cry Out Bingo: "Let's change the energy!"

4. Effect

I love skimming stones. I love the skip and hop of the circular stone on the shimmering water – an exhilarating and continuous effect – before the stone subtly slips away to the depths, having created beauty.

Lots of management books talk about 'how to make an impact'. It feels singular, a bit 'me' not 'we' - and one moment in time. Of course, it means adding value in chunks. But the word impact makes me think of a comet, hurtling towards a terminal landing site.

Could we all be more like the skimming stone? Gracefully gliding in to create positive effect, with purpose, using our power wisely to leave something remarkable behind. We'd all experience the ripple effect beyond the initial splash.

Live for Effect: Be clear on your vision and your wider purpose to create a positive ripple – a chain reaction of high performance, continuous growth and full creative flow. Know that the initial splash is only Act I. Make Effect a priority with good people, doing good work.

Cry Out Bingo: "Let's do something extraordinary!"

5. Ergonomic

Embrace and apply the *principle* of an ergonomic life. Visualise yourself bouncing around in ergonomic bliss – with an intentional style, space and energy to suit you. Minimise physical discomfort and effort – and feel in flow. Make sure you are in a space to which you are well suited. Remove barriers to bump off. Wear clothes to sprint or feel in. You want to be fluid, creative, nimble, adaptable, fast, quick of thought, grounded in intuition and see decisions clearly.

Live for Ergonomic: Design your life - be ready to bounce from adversity. Create space to regenerate and restore. Build in comfort, reduce effort, minimise fatigue - keep moving and stay in the easy zone. Like wearing your favourite trainers to meet the Greek gods.

Cry Out Bingo: "The ergos are all wrong!"

6. Efficiency

So often, I look around me and think 'this could be more efficient.'. Don't you? Wasted time and talk. Covid trained us to 'over-meet' – on-screen presenteeism is rife.

Efficiency demands constant change and reinvention – to spot shortcuts, identify quality, stay true to the vision. Developing a collaborative, well thought through, intended outcome creates clarity and an outcome anchor.

So many practices to create speed don't always work. Agile scrums and sprints can add layers of language and complication - "I think it's a load of bollocks", is muttered.

Amazon work backwards. An approach that isn't so unusual actually, in my practice of working with teams to deliver bold new offers and growth dreams.

Efficiency comes ultimately by staying in flow with your eyes on the prize.

Live for Efficiency: Watch out for efficiency killers! Call out turbulence – you're not wrong. Change things up, keep pace – stay in flow.

Cry Out Bingo: "Let's cut to the chase!"

7. Empathy

The greatest of human traits. Empathy is an invitation to collaborate to reach a higher connection and understanding. I'm not sure how we could operate without it – but dialling it up creates better performance.

Evidence shows that it is a superpower – and it can be developed and worked, like any other practised skill. And it must be rewarded, recognised and incentivised. If we choose love and have intention in our interaction – empathy will naturally feature in how we connect.

Further, can you actually feel how someone else feels – and absorb those emotions? If you are an empath, you might feel another person's emotion even before they do. Have you an empath on your team or are close to someone who might be one? Take time to understand what that means for that person – you have a Super Hero in your midst. Give space for their unique skill to help everyone. Remember Troi in Star Trek...?

Live for **Empathy:** Critical skill. Fine tune the habit. Spot a lack of empathy? Ask questions to tease it. If you are an empath, don't hide - understand it – and tell people about your natural ability.

Cry Out Bingo: "How do you feel about this?"

~

So, what do you think? Can we all forge our way towards Love Leadership? Is continuous growth and creative flow, coming from a place of love, the way to live our lives and show up at work?

There are so many sources of leadership and management learning. Gurus, coaches, advisers give us advice on how to be. It can be polarising – work like a woman, lead like a man, create feng shui in business.

Not so long ago, I agreed to take part in a podcast. Josh Nixon, from Label Sessions, raised the magic word – love – and asked me – as a marketer – about 'word of heart marketing'. I took the opportunity to talk about the importance of love in business. About 14,000 people watched it. Was that because people agreed or disagreed?

At the end of the day, we are all human beings and therefore it is love that makes the world go around. It is what inspires us and motivates to connect and create. If we trust in that – it will get the best results.

I call for an intuitive, love led approach – that is accessible to all and for all.

Choose to choose love. Are you with me?

"People, all over the world, join in, start a love train, love train"

— LOVE TRAIN, THE O'JAYS. GO PLAY IT. TRY TO
RESIST.

ABOUT THE AUTHOR
REBECCA HAMILTON

Rebecca Hamilton is a brand experience strategist, C-Suite marketer and business fast growth expert. She helps people and businesses grow quickly by creating action around an authentic, compelling story to generate brand love. Her established formula combines transformative change with creative flow leadership to deliver collaborative, 'joy-filled' results. Having achieved award winning work with some of the world's greatest memory making experience businesses, Rebecca launched her own to work in partnership with like-minded people. She is the founder of Big Brand Love, co-founder of good*SHIFT* and a Fellow of the CIM, IDM and a Leader of The Marketing Society. She loves practising growth daily through fitness, spiritual and wellbeing practice, is grateful for inspirational family and friends, and adores music, cooking - and life. Rebecca believes in creating a better world by the power of love in business, society and how we live our lives. As such, her mantra is always choose love.

- You can connect with Rebecca on LinkedIn linkedin.com/in/rebeccachamilton

- Explore her work at bigbrand.love

- Or you can find her living her life on insta' at @becshammy

4

CAR CRASH MUCH? IT'S NEVER TOO LATE TO LEARN HOW TO ENJOY A SMOOTH RIDE IN LIFE...

BERYL PREUSCHMANN

I want to chat about life as a journey, picturing it like the road you cruise your life's car along, with your destination as your secure, loved, and cozy "house" where you can just be yourself.

Let me take you through my life's wild ride - spoiler alert: it was full of bumps and twists - and share the lessons I've picked up along the way so that maybe you can have a smoother journey than mine.

Reflecting on my life, it's evident I took the trial and error route, cruising down the path to see where it leads, often ending up crashing the car, not just once, but multiple times. Each tumble was a lesson learned the hard way, making me a bit wiser each time. Now, I wonder - what if someone had shared some advice upfront to dodge these crashes? Or is crashing inevitable for personal growth? In the end, you can be the judge, but let's break it down step by step first.

Brought up in a nurturing family, I embraced my parents' beliefs without a second thought. In my teens, I had this fixed idea of school, university, back to school (I wanted to teach maths and chemistry), then family – sounds a bit silly now, doesn't it?

At 21, I had an epiphany that I was off track. But transitioning wasn't as simple as it seemed. And that's how my journey kicked off.

How did I go from "naive and silly" to "wise and still silly" (remember, humour is key) through a ton of clumsy steps because the fast-track button wouldn't cooperate?

~

Beryl's ride - the time lapse version

So without properly thinking it through I developed this way of "dealing with life", and this is "how I rolled" so to say...

I went by the Trial and Error method and adjusted things only when they got really bad, but not before. In hindsight you could probably say I proved the following proverb true: "When the student is ready - the teacher will come".

So on many occasions I simply wasn't *ready* to learn what life was trying to teach me. I was stubborn and persevered to the point of breaking. And then I rebuilt myself so to say - like a phoenix from the ashes... And I am really not so sure if that was the only way to do it - and I am pretty sure it's not the healthiest way to do it either... This is somehow the seemingly eternal loop I found myself in:

1. Feeling uneasy - readjust path
2. Along the new path: find new parts of self
3. Adjust values
4. Still didn't get it right - car crash
5. Rise from the ashes - be inspirational - go back to a.

And that procedure, as you will see, somehow went on for quite a while like a merry-go-round - and I finally introduced a new step ***F - Ask for help / advice*** and more importantly - asked myself what I truly truly wanted and started to listen to my inner voice and respected my inner feelings and started to finally love myself.

So to avoid sounding too technical here, I thought I'd try and put my life into chapters to show you what the merry-go-round looked like.

PART I - From Berlin uni life to studying in Ireland

I stayed at home for my first two years at university because I was too scared to tell my parents I wanted my own space. Slowly, I started feeling uneasy and knew I had to make a change. When I was 22 I decided to study abroad and ditched plans for Australia in favour of a year at Trinity College in Dublin, where I already had friends. My mum saw through my plan to escape home life, which taught me the lesson of being honest about my intentions to avoid awkward situations.

My year in Ireland was a transformative experience that shook up my emotions and redefined my life. Immersed in a new setting, I found myself seen through a different lens, where traditional markers of success like academic achievements lost their meaning. Adjusting to a slower pace of conversation and a shift in how my identity was perceived, I realised the power of genuine expression over superficial facades. In this new environment, pretence fell away, allowing me to discover my true self without the constraints of my past reputation. While I no longer had the luxury of relying on familiar accolades, I embraced the freedom to define my own identity, exploring personal style and hobbies to shape a new me.

PART II - Return to Berlin - find self by doing anything but studying

In Berlin, my focus on science and achievement led me to embrace a tomboy persona, but in Dublin, I yearned to rediscover my teenage self, seeking to experience girlhood and test my boundaries. This journey involved a blend of challenging and rewarding encounters, marked by tears, phone calls back home (it was the time before email...) - But every time my mum suggested I come home I felt stronger in my refusal - I wanted to test this out. I wanted to grow up...

So I would say the first steps of self-awareness were definitely made in this period in my early to mid-20s. People pleasing slowly shifted the wish to like myself first and find out what I liked about myself to start with. But like Bambi, my legs were still a bit shaky, so on my return to Berlin what changes did I make and why were they half-arsed (pardon my French), maybe I should say half-bollocksed having come back from Ireland? Firstly I didn't move back into my parental home after coming back! Tick. But what did I do instead - I moved in with my boyfriend. Can you see the irony? I wanted to live by myself but was too scared to actually do it so I moved in with a new point of reference... So again I didn't listen to my true feelings - I made a decision out of fear - the fear of being lonely, the fear of not belonging... Did it work out? Of course not - who was I kidding - but it was nice while it lasted... Another lesson learnt - *beep*!

So in another close to car crash move - at the age of 27, to gain independence, I took on a job as a waitress alongside my university studies, working late nights and early mornings. It revealed my entrepreneurial side, providing financial freedom but was clearly also becoming a diversion from my studies. In the lax academic environment of 90s Germany, many students attended university in name only, prioritising social life over academics. Lost in this drift, I left my boyfriend to strike out on my own, only to fall deeply in love with a new man, throwing my emotions into turmoil. The highs and lows of this tumultuous romance coupled with my career indecision, really set me out for my next car crash. This time my emotions tumbled lower and lower and I was out for a big one. So much so that I finally realised I needed some proper guidance and help.

And for this step I am forever grateful to myself. I got up and *asked for help*. I sought out counselling.

PART III - Finish new degree and work in cool TV environment

As proud as I am that I acknowledged my need for guidance and reflection, it didn't go straight onward from here. Of course - I think we established that by now...

With the help of my new counsellor I established what I wanted in the future... A job that is fun and involves working with people, would embrace the beauty of life and would inspire others. I wanted a husband and four kids - well more than two I think, kids not husbands. The desire to have kids was very very clear.

But I was also a very impatient person, in a way, I just couldn't wait for things to evolve - once I have an idea I push it through.

So once I had established that becoming a teacher wasn't for me anymore - even though it ticked a few of the new found boxes I had manifested - I felt free, so I thought I'd rush through the exams to at least finish my degree so that I could start with a new career path straight after... And like in the mentioned proverb - I the student was ready - so teachers came and they taught me and lent a helping hand along the way... One of these supportive figures remains my best friend to this day.

But subconsciously I sabotaged myself again... I think the fear of ending up in the same rut yet again was too great - so I gloriously failed my exams and closed that path for good... another car crash so to say... but by then I was quite used to them and without even hesitating I got up - brushed myself off and moved on. Aged 30, a chance encounter with a university advisor, who seemed to understand me effortlessly, led me to enrol in Electronic Business studies. This decision, guided by her wisdom, opened up a new path that eventually led me to where I am today.

Transitioning to Electronic Business, a blend of design, business studies, and computer science, allowed my creative and entrepreneurial sides to flourish. Embracing my inner stage hog, I excelled in presentations, forming a dream team with friends who excelled in research and design. I never had the patience for detailed research nor the genius of a true designer. I loved the beauty of it all and my scientific brain loved the details, but it turns out I am the front woman - the one who spins the yarn. This dynamic continued as we navigated through university, with one friend still a close companion today.

After finally finishing my degree, life led me to a fulfilling career as an online editor at a top German TV station.

This gig turned out to be something truly awesome. I remember picturing during my counselling sessions a job that would inspire others, involve picturesque settings, and teamwork. I'm all about people and storytelling. Surprisingly, each job I landed after that matched these ideals, even though they were all quite different. I rocked this role, liaising with the production crew, actors, and the TV station itself. I took a different approach, crossing boundaries and connecting all the dots to craft a story that worked for everyone involved. It was a fantastic time. However, all good things must come to an end. The TV station decided to relocate to Munich, leading to a gradual downsizing of operations in Berlin.

The merry-go-round of new beginnings to crash seemed to become faster... but I became more and more seasoned in my reaction to these events.

PART IV - Go to Scotland - be inspirational

With my newfound attitude, I wasn't fazed at all about losing my job. I remember expressing to a friend my wish to be handed my notice on the following Monday, and miraculously, it came true. Shortly before, I had a conversation at a friend's wedding that sparked the idea of visiting them in Scotland, a place that had captured my heart years ago. The same Monday, I was put on gardening leave, and by Friday, I found myself in Scotland for a two-week exploratory journey to rekindle my connection with the country. The allure remained, prompting a swift decision to move to Edinburgh. Despite suggestions for Glasgow, because of the media connections, an inner voice guided me firmly towards Edinburgh, I just somehow knew it was right for me. And finally I seemed to have been able to hear my inner voices and trusted my instincts. And without properly knowing why and how - at the age of 35 I packed my bags, sublet my flat and moved to Edinburgh, surprising many friends and colleagues. My parents were truly supportive even though it was probably not what they had envisaged for me and for that I am also forever grateful.

And even though so many had been surprised by my move, most of my closest friends weren't surprised at all because they too could feel the strong pull that called me to Scotland and they could feel that my decision was completely aligned with my wishes. And in later years I received numerous emails and messages from

44

acquaintances and colleagues who had looked at my move with curious eyes, sharing how they too had taken the leap to new places or roles, inspired by my journey. These messages continue to bring me joy, as they reinforce the importance of pursuing your dreams, intuitions, and feelings without fear.

PART V - Try a couple of different corporate environments

You're not expecting a straight road ahead, right? It felt like home, Scotland, but I was still finding my voice, a bit naive and silly. In counselling, I identified key attributes that blended naturally in Edinburgh and Scotland: inspirational, beautiful, vibrant, free-spirited, earthy, optimistic, collaborative. Joining VisitScotland aligned with my love for the country, emphasising storytelling with diverse individuals, enriching the experience. Yet, as my personality evolved, corporate roles felt increasingly mismatched; I yearned to break free from conformity and infuse my personal touch into everything. So I went and crashed the car one more time...

PART VI - Go self-employed

In essence, after realising I wouldn't fit into a corporate setting despite valuing teamwork, at the age of 40 I found my calling in Scotland's aesthetic and beauty-centred roles. Taking the self-employed route was a natural step, allowing me the freedom to make choices based on how I felt. This path aligns with nurturing my love for Scotland's beauty and sharing it with others, connecting to my desire to educate and guide through tours and trip planning. It's more than showcasing scenic spots - it's about building a network of like-minded individuals and delving into Scotland's essence.

PART VII - Find self-love

Remember how I said I wanted a family and I wanted four kids? Well I had gotten my career on path - but on the romantic side I was nowhere nearer to that idea of a family life than ten years beforehand. So I just went by my own new rules and went back to counselling and admitted I had clearly not found the path to my envisaged family life yet so I needed to find that path. I asked for help and guidance... Firstly on a quest to finally love myself first and foremost.

Counselling truly peels back the layers of your emotional onion. It's been a revealing journey; I've become calmer, emotionally mature, and more balanced. The key lesson learned is to be my own best friend, valuing self-love and self-acceptance over seeking external validation. This mindset shift culminated in a pivotal moment at a friend's wedding, where I embraced my single status without reservation, content in my own company. At 45 years old, I had finally grown up inside.

That same summer - literally in the same week, I bought my first house for investment, treated myself to my first car, and met my now-husband. It was a moment of significant personal and financial milestones. I believe in living life on my own timeline, not bound by societal expectations of when certain milestones should be reached.

PART VIII - Start family

Now, five years later, I have my own family - two lovely daughters, one born when I was 47, and the other at 49. The journey to parenthood was a testament to perseverance and refusing to accept defeat. By exploring alternative paths and embracing the help of an egg donor, we defied the odds to achieve our desired outcome. In both pregnancies, I challenged the conventional notions of older mothers and overdue babies, proving that healthy pregnancies can extend to 43 weeks. The second birth, a serene home birth, exemplified my commitment to doing things on my terms.

As for the four-kids-plan, well, that's a question better posed to the husband! Personally, I'd be all in for another one if you ask me!

∼

So how could it be done better?

Be true to yourself and own your emotions - be in charge - trust life and yourself

In sharing my chaotic tale, I hope I was able to encourage you and others to embrace and appreciate your unique journey, diverging from societal norms and expectations. Remember, your life is yours to navigate, your truth to uncover, and your contentment to prioritise.

I clearly don't claim to have all the answers or a flawless life, but through self-discovery, self-acceptance, and kindness, I've found a sense of fulfilment and joy. Each twist and turn has led me to this point of contentment, where I've embraced the unpredictability of life and the unexpected turns it brings.

This isn't a quick-fix self-help guide; it's a journey filled with twists and turns, a reminder to retain your sense of wonder and humour, and to relish every moment of the adventure. Life is a thrilling ride, please simply enjoy it!! And the discoveries and encounters along the way are what make it truly amazing. I'm eagerly anticipating what lies ahead, fuelled by curiosity and excitement for the next chapter.

If I were to revamp the wild ride of chaos plan I had listed in the earlier part of the chapter - the one I've embraced all these years, here's the updated game plan for you:

1. Stay in tune with yourself
2. Continuously recalibrate your course
3. Reaffirm and adapt your core values
4. Inspire others along the way
5. Embrace seeking guidance without fear
6. Delight in a smoother journey

ABOUT THE AUTHOR
BERYL PREUSCHMANN

Beryl Preuschmann is the CEO and founder of Trip Organiser
Scotland. She curates exceptional travel experiences, guiding clients
to explore Scotland's hidden gems and beyond. Born and raised in
Berlin, Germany, Beryl's academic journey from Mathematics and
Chemistry to Electronic Business reflects her resilient spirit. As the
daughter of an entrepreneurial mother, Beryl was instilled with a
strong and spirited background from a young age. After a successful
period as an online editor for a top-rated telenovela and TV station,
she felt the call to Scotland. Beginning as a temporary worker with
the NHS, Beryl swiftly advanced to roles as an online editor and PR
Manager at VisitScotland. This diverse background served as the
foundation for her entrepreneurial venture, culminating in the
establishment of TRIPorganiser Scotland. Her journey embodies a
fusion of determination, adaptability, and a profound love for

creating unforgettable adventures. Beryl lives in the heart of Edinburgh now. She's never once looked back...

- https://triporganiser.net
- https://linktr.ee/triporganiser
- https://www.instagram.com/miss_beryl/

5

CLAIMING LOVE

MEL PECK

The magic that transforms our soul is when we dare to embrace our most loving, and brightest self.

— *MEL PECK*

Cliff edge. You find me sitting on a rocky outcrop overlooking the English Channel. It's a blue-sky crisp day. Early signs of Spring are emerging with the odd pink campion and daffodil shoot. Suddenly the wind whips up and reminds me it's still Winter...earmuffs on. Staring out into the blue I realise I have manifested everything I asked for into being. I am living my best life. I feel a heady mix of freedom, relief, wonderful exhaustion, and excitement. I am exactly where I am meant to be.

To get here I have invested in women's coaching, become a trauma informed professional, had my heart utterly shattered, been temporarily paralysed on an intercity train, returned to university, resigned from my substantive job, moved countries...twice, and started my own business. Oh, and somewhere during all that I turned 40!

But this was no mid-life crisis. These were the most conscious decisions and catalysts for change in my life I have ever taken and experienced. My most challenging awakening yet. The destination? Claiming love as my superpower.

Metamorphosis. So, you might be thinking...love...yea right! But love is certainly not the easy path to take. Fluffy bunnies exit left now. Learning to trust in living and leading with conscious loving intention required a complete metamorphosis. Like the butterfly, who must pass through the phases of egg, caterpillar, and chrysalis before emerging as an adult, I too had to experience different (and painful) but necessary stages. I had to let go of my life as I knew it and awaken to the possibilities of the life that was waiting for me.

Still in? This is my story.

Good egg

You cannot go on indefinitely being just an ordinary, decent egg. We must be hatched or go bad.

— C. S. LEWIS

A good egg. I have always known that I have an extraordinary capacity for love. Love has always walked loyally by my side. I attribute this to growing up in an idyllic carefree (and screen free) childhood with the full complement of loving parents, adoring grandparents, and supportive family. I spent these years climbing trees, hand-rearing goslings, and jumping in streams in my bridesmaid's dress. I loved it. The stars gifted me with Sagittarian eternal optimism, enthusiasm, amiability, an insatiable quest for knowledge and passion for helping others. An all-round *good egg*.

Change. But in the world beyond my family love often became my biggest vulnerability. As a 90's teenager my passions were viewed as uncool, childish, or nerdy. At university being kind led to complex social situations. One by one the way I expressed love and what I loved were pushed down. I learnt to hide love behind learning and academia.

Born to be a speechy. Thankfully, on the advice of a dear friend, I enrolled in a degree in speech and language therapy. What a decision this was to be. Four years later I qualified into one of the most diverse, creative, enigmatic, and deeply neuroscientific professions. Genuinely, we transform lives. Two decades later I remain incredibly proud and fiercely passionate about speech therapy. My career has taken me around the globe working across the lifespan advocating for the single most important essence of being human, the right to have a voice.

Appearing perfect. Fifteen years later and I had been commuting on a daily four-hour round trip to my *dream job* for five years. Yes, four hours. So, you might be thinking... *"Wow you must really love your job"*. And in many respects, I did. I had reached a pinnacle in my career. A clinical lead at a major children's hospital. I was creating my vision of restructuring the service and had doubled the size of the team through sheer perseverance. I was realising my dream of sharing knowledge through teaching, training, and publishing work. Everything appeared perfect.

Going bad? But despite a deep love and dedication to my work and clients something wasn't right. And it wasn't the commute. I felt increasingly out of step at work. An unsettling discomfort with the way people spoke and behaved. At first, I shrugged this off, decided to stick to what I knew best and be a *good egg.* I dutifully committed to creating a C.V bulging with achievements, qualifications, and certifications and completed managerial tasks in, (as we say in my family), *"overachiever"* style. But I couldn't shake off the discomfort. I felt caught in a toxic creeping culture of corporate competitiveness, overconfidence and entitlement.

Silenced voice. I was watching from the sidelines in a tri-pincer grip. My profession was being shoehorned into a healthcare model of impairment and prescription. Ironically, for a speechy I felt my voice wasn't being heard. Worse still I knew those without a voice (our clients and families) could not be heard either. The final crusher was, it wasn't just me. I was hearing from incredibly gifted colleagues far and wide in overwhelm and burn out. The fallout of squeezing a linguistically artistic profession into a medical model may well be the creation of an astonishingly resilient workforce. But it is also one that ends up soaking up every other systemically engrained shortcoming and becomes compassion fatigued. Something had to change. Hatch or go bad.

~

Larva

There is nothing in a caterpillar that tells you it's going to be a butterfly.

— R BUCKMINSTER FULLER

Caterpillar. When butterfly eggs hatch, tiny caterpillars (larva) emerge and begin feeding and growing. As they eat their bodies expand and their skin becomes tight and eventually splits and sheds, revealing new skin beneath. This moulting occurs several times as the larva grows.

Hatching. It's May 2020. The middle of a global pandemic. Lockdown. And I was searching. The voice in my head was switched on repeat with an unshakeable thought that I was meant to be doing *something else*. But whatever this voice was trying to tell me, I couldn't hear it clearly. I was working crazy hours trying my best to guide my team through uncharted COVID water. All whilst feeling confused, in friction with myself but most of all guilty that I was at the top of my game and thinking, "*Is this it?*"

Catalyst. That's when I met Mel MacIntyre, my coach and curator of this book. I'd been listening to her webinars and found myself compelled to reach out to her. During a half-hour phone call she was able to identify with every thought I was having. I wasn't alone. I remember thinking, this is completely mad, I don't know this woman. But I decided to leap. I signed up to her *Becoming Wildly Authentic*™ coaching programme. I had no idea what I was doing or that this would be the catalyst to a series of *moults* in my life.

Hungry caterpillar. The programme was intense. But I was in...*all in.* I was hungry to grow. I started with making the small changes we *all* talk about but never do. Everything from drinking more water, weekly yoga, running to and from the train station. I started optimising my 'power hour' at work and was quickly redirecting and reclaiming my energy through creating clear boundaries. I was adapting to a new mindset. Retraining my reactive mind to a responsive one...care less, love more.

Moulting. I started outwardly expressing what I loved and how I felt joy. I was remembering all the things that made me, me. I could finally hear my own voice. Like the caterpillar, I was shedding layers of old narratives. A generational guilt of how I should be living my life as a woman...something many of the amazing women on the programme also felt. But in this protected haven we could become our most authentic, unapologetic self. I was openly realising my truth. I wrote down every dream I had ever had. I went BIG. I knew my worth. And I *was* worthy of more.

Clarity. The quiet voice which had been stuffed inside the shell of a *good egg* was hatched, nourished, and squawking loudly. And with urgent clarity. Within three months of the programme, I had dropped a day at work, registered as a sole trader and enrolled on a new global training programme. I knew the change I was searching for wasn't outside of me, it was within me. In fact, it *was* me. I loved my profession and I had to help. Love was my superpower. Now to claim it.

Chrysalis

Nothing happens until the pain of remaining the same outweighs the pain of change.

— ARTHUR BURT

Pupa. When the caterpillar has grown enough, it finds a protective place and moults for the last time to form a chrysalis (pupa) in which they metamorphose. The pupa undergoes immense change as the caterpillar dissolves into a "tissue cell soup" developing new body parts. When the butterfly emerges, its metamorphosis is complete.

Shattered into pieces. Of course, it wasn't going to be easy. Two weeks after my coaching finished, the love of my life walked out of my life. My person just left. No warning. Blindsided. Shock ripped through my body in repeated battering waves. Knocked again and again in disbelief. Waking night upon night screaming. Soaked in never-ending tears. A twisted and relentless grip around my heart so tight I had to fight to find breath. It made no sense, other than his sense. Utterly distraught. My soul was ripped apart.

Then the silence.

Chrysalised.

Darkness. Throughout my life people have often commented on my light. That I bring sunshine into the room. A light in the darkness. The strange thing about being in my own darkness when I'm naturally filled with light is that I could always feel the light but knew it was going to take me an incredibly long time to reach it again. I knew my own heart and felt exhausted at the prospect. A second national lockdown added a raw social isolation. But there was no other choice. I knew I had to wait it out in the darkness...however long she stayed.

Blackout. It's 7:30 am. I've been back at work for a week. I'm on my daily commute in an empty train carriage, mid pandemic. From nowhere I feel searing pains shooting through all my limbs. Like hot pokers. I have a muscle condition. But this was new. I was in trouble. I was having an acute attack. I'd never experienced anything like it. My body was rapidly shutting down. Within seconds I was completely paralysed. Blackout.

SOS. By luck my phone was on my lap, and with my wrist somehow, I dialled home. Dad answered. Next I remember a station guard walking toward me with that look of... *"who's this nutter?"* But leaning in his eyes turned grim as he realised I was like a ragdoll. Dad had managed to get in touch with our specialist nurse, who said, don't go to the hospital. I had to get home. My parents were snowed in. We were in lockdown. After an SOS to my dear friends, a few hours later I was wheeled off the train. When I saw their faces, I could barely contain my tears. They knew exactly what to do. I felt so loved. But it was a shocking wake up call. I was deep in the darkness.

Becoming a Trauma Informed Professional™. They say life is all about timing. Unexpected guidance through my darkness came from another incredible woman, Mary Coughlin, and her team. By luck I had already enrolled on a programme of learning where love and compassion were centre stage. I couldn't believe it. I was devouring the science behind the soul of everything I believed. Loud bells were ringing. This was my harmony. It wasn't just me. The suppressed compassion, silent friction, and toxic medicalised competition was real. And like any trauma it was pervasively seeping through every aspect of healthcare.

Healing. For me the greatest gift of this time was in the reflection it allowed me. Becoming trauma informed starts with us hearing our own truth, and for me I found the strength of my own healing presence. I allowed myself to feel my sadness and consciously and compassionately care for myself with absolute love. I became adept at noticing and feeling grateful for little moments. A robin's song. A ladybird in Winter. The months and months and months of sobbing down the phone (at all hours) to my incredibly patient friends and family (yes, *you*) were healing waters. But I remember letting out a wimpy cheer the first time I'd boiled the kettle and hadn't cried. My light was coming back.

If not now, when? If not you, who? At work I found a new level of connection with others. It was as if my intuition to *be with* others had become supercharged. I was listening with a new ability to *hear*. I was listening *with love and a compassionate presence*. I was not just happy opening Pandora's box, I was actively looking inside it. And once again I felt that call *"...if not now, when? If not you, who?"* is going to be their voice?

∿

Butterfly

Things do not change. We change.

— HENRY THORE

Wet winged. Somewhere in a lighter shade of darkness I emerged. Barely recognisable. I had changed. I can't remember a lot about that time but knew instinctively I had to start writing. I became determined to create a new learning experience. One that went beyond theory and skills. One that nurtured the very soul of intentional change. One that cut down into the uncomfortable topics eating away at my profession. I reached out to my peers announcing a new online clinical coaching programme. In one week, five beautiful souls sign up. I was hanging in suspension, like a new butterfly, waiting. Could I really do this? Wet winged, I took flight.

Flying. Eight programmes later I have reached nearly 60 clinicians and expanded my unique pedagogy into university. The feedback has been life affirming. Months later I still receive messages demonstrating that just little me leading with love, sharing what I love and believing in that love creates a ripple effect. It turns out that when we connect through our deepest individual fears and vulnerabilities, we realise these are our collective fears. But together we can look with our understanding to face them with compassionate presence, and collaboratively create the change we want to see.

Higher altitude. I didn't stop there. I took sabbatical leave and scratched my itch to go back to university. What I didn't predict was how being catapulted (picture Alice on a sling-slot) down this post-grad rabbit hole would ignite my brain! Comparative and evolutionary perspectives allowed me not only to continue to reflect on how *I* got here but explore with deep curiosity how *we* got here i.e., the story of our shared human heritage. And how this shaped the narrative of modern human ways of thinking, feeling, and behaving.

My bonobo teacher. One animal who captured and fuelled my passion was the bonobo *(Pan paniscus)*. Their social structure is matriarchal i.e., led by females. Relationships are based on reciprocity, a trusted co-operation and where *"genito-genital rubbing"* (if you get my gist) maintains peace. Of importance, the bonobo is *equally* our closest living cousin, alongside the chimpanzee *(Pan troglodytes)*. That means that the origin of *humans* can and has also evolved through societies which not only survive, but thrive through love, trust, and cooperation, led by females. It's an interesting coincidence that their classification as a distinct species of great ape from chimpanzees, only came in 1929, a year after women won the right to vote in the UK.

Be more bonobo. Whilst Victorian Britain was rightly celebrating equal rights for women, the Darwinian history books conveniently overlooked a shockingly biased and incorrect skewing of our ancestral phylogeny. The favoured (and historically funded) narrative of our evolutionary heritage has been consistently pitched as originating from patriarchal chimpanzees who lead through male dominance, aggression, and competition. Sound familiar? As I look at the world around us, I wonder how much this has shaped a modern human cultural landscape devoid of love, trust, or collaboration.

What could it look like if we were all more bonobo?

Butterflies rising

Feel everything that is beautiful and possible in your soul and let yourself become it.

— BUTTERFLIES RISING

Urgency. For me, my metamorphosis did not just change me but it gave me the courage to be the change. I refocused my lens to live with loving intention and now constantly re-phrase the classic medical question of *"what's wrong with you?"* to a trauma informed one of *"what happened to you?"* However, I believe we must now extend this and recognise with haste *"what happened to us?"* We must look back with our understanding and learn from trans-millennial trauma to truly address how modern humans won't just survive but thrive into the future. Now more than ever I am working with an urgency to role model and integrate teaching frameworks nurturing foundational attributes of connection, compassion, and collaboration to ensure a professionally responsive, trauma-informed, and confident profession who will lead and live with love.

No apology. Speech and language therapy (thankfully) will never be the adrenalin pumped showy sprinters of the healthcare world. We have little interest in crossing the line first, fastest or bolstered by an array of drugs. We won't ever fit into a system where bragging rights for *"being busy"* or favouring quantity over quality models work for us. Neither do our core values or the complexity of therapeutic interventions fit into dichotomous outcomes of *"speech vs no speech"* or *"safe vs unsafe swallow"*. No, we are more akin to steeplechase runners, here for the long haul. We reflect a diverse and brilliantly talented group of humans who persevere with dynamic flexibility in balancing an extraordinary set of spinning plates. Uniquely skilled to *see it all*, our work takes time, because it requires love, and compassionate presence. And we don't ever need to apologise for that.

Claiming love. Love is not without painful loss and grief. Love is not without days, months, (and years) of grappling culturally ingrained narratives of what or who you should be. Love is not without daily fear of rejection, self-doubt, or animosity from others. Love is not without deep exposure to vulnerability, misinterpretation, or making mistakes. Claiming love is facing all of this, regardless of the outcome, because it is the right path to choose.

> *"When I leave, I want to say,*
> *Rising up, I shared my light.*
> *I was loved. And I loved big.*
> *But the real truth is, I lived."*

ABOUT THE AUTHOR
MEL PECK

Mel Peck is a multi-passionate certified speech and language therapist and trauma informed professional™. Her bespoke coaching programmes inspire clinicians to transform their practice through connection, compassion, and collaboration guiding confident decision-making.

As a developmental and acquired communication and swallowing specialist with two decades of clinical experience she has held substantive leadership roles in UK healthcare. Mel is a regular guest lecturer at City University, has collaborated with the London Symphony Orchestra using music as a medium for learning and wellbeing and, led the development and publication of new therapy outcome measures and evidence-based care.

Her mission is to ensure the future of her beloved profession by role modelling and teaching a salutogenic model of healthcare. Without any apology for the time, skill, artistry, and humanity required to transform the lives of those with communication and swallowing difficulties.

Mel lives in Suffolk surrounded by loving friends and family and supported by a global sisterhood of compassionate activists.

- To find out more about Mel's work please visit https://www.melstinytalkers.co.uk or email melstinytalkers@gmail.com

6

LIVING AND LEADING 'THE LEMON WAY'!

JENNIFER LEMON

My version of 'Awakened Leadership' is still a work in progress.

I can't pretend to be a) calm, b) enlightened or c) good at yoga.

In fact, I'm none of these things.

I prefer coffee to green tea, I switch between procrastination and perfectionism and I'm more gin than gym. You get the picture.

And yet, now, at my middling 46 years, running my own business and my own home, I feel more alive, more content and more 'awake' than ever. I'm in my Lemon era and I'm absolutely here for it.

So how did I get here?

I was born Jennifer Lemon on a balmy Saturday in July in the late 70's. The middle daughter of a middle-class family, I was imaginative, expressive, and emotional. From a very early age I was self-conscious and aware - quick to tears and quick to laughter.

Yet despite my sensitivity and soft exterior, I've always had a steely strength. A resilience. Pith. I affectionately call it my 'Lemon Spirit'.

I was a mainly placid child, yet in the playground my Lemon spirit gave me an inner-knowing to understand what was right, wrong, kind or mean. Founded upon my family values, it gave me the courage to stick up for myself and my friends, the passion to fight against unfairness and the wit to outsmart the boys.

We were 'The Lemons'; my family lived in the 'middle of nowhere' in a Worcestershire cottage surrounded by open green fields, with the nearest neighbour over half a mile away in both directions. I spent many happy hours with my two sisters riding our bikes, making dens, going over the fields and playing with our dogs and cats, and my hundreds of teddies and Sindy dolls. My entrepreneurial parents ran – and still run - their own business manufacturing and retailing traditional oils and polishes for wood finishing which are shipped all over the world. My Dad – brimming with Lemon Spirit - was always going to be his own boss. I learned how to make money from skills and ideas. I enjoyed earning pocket money by helping package the products. At the weekend, I loved going to the video shop with my Dad and I soaked up the fairytales and myths of 'True Love's Kiss', 'love at first sight' and 'happily ever after' watching Disney, and many an 80's film.

As I grew up, I fully bought into the idea that if I worked hard, told the truth, treated others kindly and stayed positive, my life would follow a set pattern: school-A-Levels-University-Marriage-Kids-Happily Ever After in a little cottage with roses around the door.

My first chapters seemed to follow the expected path - I did study hard, I did well at school, won drama trophies, covered my Guides uniform in badges, achieved a clutch of A-Levels and met my husband-to-be during Freshers' Week at Uni. Married at 25, child at 30 – everything perfectly on schedule. Life was good - so far, so Disney.

But in the real world, most of us have had our share of (bitter) lemons hurled at us by our forties and mine came in threes:

Chronic illness, redundancy, divorce...

In that order.

These three lemons shattered my life in a way that even a Fairy Godmother wouldn't be able to fix...

Bitter lemon #1 - illness

Whilst I've painted a blissful picture of my childhood, of course there were blips and I started suffering from migraines and anxiety in my teens. The migraines got worse and after pregnancy, for some reason, my health plummeted. Severe migraines had me bed-bound with pain and sickness for days on end, episodes of depression and overwhelm, chronic fatigue and days where I suffered all over itching and inflammation. As I reached 40, the symptoms became worse and worse. I struggled with maintaining a stressful job in the City, whilst masking my illness, and balancing a young child, husband and home, whilst trying to maintain the appearance of a perfect life - keeping everything 'Disney-fied'. I was convinced that my cyclical symptoms indicated that my illness was hormone related. I went to countless specialists - none of whom could pinpoint a diagnosis. I continued to suffer month in, month out whilst I jumped through many hoops seeking a referral for a hysterectomy.   Despite understanding the risks of surgery, I felt it was worth the chance of feeling well again.

Bitter lemon #2 - redundancy

At around the same time that I was struggling with my health, I found myself in a division of my organisation which was very male-focused, and I became more and more unhappy with the culture. There was misogynistic banter, inappropriate comments about my legs and a senior male staff member regularly 'bumping into me'. At our divisional networking event, I was asked how my mostly female team would be able to deliver on our IT programme as there would likely be so much "time lost due to pregnancies"; another time I was asked if I was the "drinks lady" on entering a meeting. I was fuming. On raising the issues with a Board Member, I received a notice of my role's redundancy the following week. I fought the notice for some time, until the situation became so challenging that I was unable to manage it alongside my health issues. After 16 successful years, I was made redundant. It was a huge dent to my self-esteem. It felt unfair and discriminatory, yet at the same time, whilst I had enjoyed some great years with the company, I felt it had become a place I didn't want to be any more. I soon found a new bid role within a training organisation, winning almost every bid I wrote on their behalf, before branching out on my own in a freelance capacity two years later.

Bitter lemon #3 - divorce

Just at the point where I'd finally got my doctors to agree to a full hysterectomy and bilateral oophorectomy to prevent my hormones driving my body and mind haywire, my husband and partner of 20 years announced, "he hadn't been happy for years" and left me for a woman from work.

I never dreamed that this could happen to me in a million years. What about my happily ever after? ...How can this be *my* story?

I was plunged into darkness.

My family, my home, my security – everything I'd always believed in – gone. Incredibly ill and with my surgery looming, I found myself in the same horrible position as many women facing divorce, having to negotiate between a pension and my home in a divorce settlement. I discovered that keeping a roof over my head meant losing my long-term financial security, and that 'child support' payments are woefully inadequate.

The pain, anger, grief – a wound so deep, I thought I would die.

All my demons legitimised. I'm not thin enough. I'm boring. I'm lazy. I'm too much; I'm not enough.

I wanted to disappear - I drank too much - I ate too little - I thought I would never get over it.

But my Dad told me. "Yes, you will get over it. You're a Lemon".

And he was right.

They say what doesn't kill you makes you stronger. For me it just made me more Lemon. When I was at my darkest, sick and sobbing, my Lemon spirit gave me the backbone and the dogged determination to carry on.

In reference to my idol Beyonce, I started 'Lemonaiding'. I funnelled my rage into showing everyone what I was made of, and I began learning how to cope. As I gained new skills, and started to heal through the help of counselling and my supporters, I began to realise that:

- I had become over-dependent upon my ex-husband. It might sound ridiculous, but I had no idea on the state of our finances – or that we had got into a lot of debt. I didn't even know how to log into my own online bank accounts or pay our household bills. I'd never taxed or insured the car or been to the tip. I'd never fixed the vacuum cleaner, changed a fuse or mowed the lawn. I hadn't even done much cooking as he had liked to cook. Suddenly, I needed to handle everything on my own. It was tough; my daughter and I punched pillows together to release our anger.

- There had been deep flaws in my marriage; living such a full-on life packed with holidays and activities and all that 'doing' was not the life I really wanted. I love holidays and I love glamour – but I also need quiet. I need alone time, pottering at home, reading the paper with my morning coffee, enjoying my garden, cuddling my cats, being silly with my daughter. These are equally important to being busy for me and this quiet time is critical for my health.

- I am capable. I created a log of household income and outgoings, account numbers and due dates. I paid the bills and was never in debt. I remortgaged the house. I changed my Will. I bought critical health and life insurance. I began to enjoy cooking again. I bought a power washer and jet-washed the patio, I tended to the garden. Each time I changed a light bulb, fixed the DVD player, added screen wash to the car, it felt like a little victory. Despite the deep feelings of shock, unfairness and loss, and the difficulty of managing my illness alongside everything else, I felt a lightness that I was now in control of my destiny. I was taking ownership of my life, and I began to feel strong.

- I love working for myself and being my own boss. I love being creative, writing and working with clients who share my enthusiasm and values. As a leader in my field, I'm now growing my business - using my skills and experience to train others. I've updated our services offer, our website and collateral and become a UK registered training provider.

- I am not lazy. I've been diagnosed with a chronic autoimmune illness which flares alongside hormonal and other fluctuations. This means that there are times every month when I feel extremely unwell and low. It isn't my fault.

- I have a huge support team of cheerleaders. Those who sent notes, delivered flowers, cooked meals, checked-in. My little sister who drove me into London for my hysterectomy and made me laugh so much about my 'sexy' medical stockings that I danced into the operating theatre. I will be forever grateful.

- I'm not too much, too fat, or too thin. Like baby bear's porridge, I'm just right.

I now see my Lemon Spirit as core to who I am. I am still a work in progress. I still procrastinate, I'm *never* going to be a gym bunny, and I love a gin and tonic. But I'm no longer sleep-walking - I'm awake. I'm in control of my life, my relationships, my business, and my feelings. With Lemon as my guide, so far, I've:

• Launched a new consulting business – Customeric Consulting LLP. We had a bumper first year and I quadrupled my salary.

• Moved to a beautiful Coach House. I hadn't planned to move, and yet this character property came on to the market just around the corner from my home. I made an offer and had it accepted. It felt fortuitous. It is a labour of love which we are renovating. There aren't roses around the door (yet!), but it sits on the River Ivel, next to Stotfold's ancient watermill, so I can watch the swans on the river from my bedroom window. This is my forever home, the cottage I've always dreamed of, and I feel peaceful and content.

• Found love again with an amazing man who loves and accepts *all* my colours. I've got older and I've become happier in my awakened, Lemony skin!

• Developed an incredibly strong bond and friendship with my daughter. Having gone through so much together, just the two of us, we are closer than ever. Apparently, I am a 'cool mum', and she's my sunshine.

• Accepted that there is no miracle cure for my illness and whilst

I'm still trialling medication, diets and balancing my hormones, sometimes I just need to listen to my body, and rest without guilt.

The good news is that because I have sucked on the plate of bitter lemons which ultimately set me on a path to changing my life for the better, I can share some of my new juicy wisdom! So here are my top 10 tips for 'living and leading the Lemon way'!

1. Tap into your inner Lemon – and use it as your guide

Your name may not be Lemon, you may be a Jones, Morgan whatever... get to know yourself – and bring that fully authentic you to the table.

Be guided and notice how you really feel about decisions, people, work. Don't be swayed by others' opinions – lean into your inner voice and do it – or don't do it - your own way.

I find that if I really listen to my intuition, I already know the answers. I now actively tune in and notice how my body feels when making a decision, and if something or someone makes me feel uncomfortable, I know they are not for me. Don't waste your fire on people or projects that are not worthy of your time, energy, or care. Move on with grace.

2. Go for it!

This is one of my Mum's favourite phrases. It's a simple message of positivity. It means believing in yourself, putting in the graft to get where you want to go and not being dissuaded by naysayers who might tell you all the reasons why your idea or dream won't work. One of my favourite poems is Wintle's, 'Thinking', "*If you think you are beaten, you are ... You've got to think high to rise*" I had to believe in myself and take a risk to start my own successful business. Sometimes you've just got to go for it.

3. Take action

"*This time next year Rodney, we'll be millionaires!*" This is a regular quote I use with my partner. We have a little laugh, but who knows? If we take the baby steps towards our dreams, perhaps they will come true! Often, we become paralysed with fear, procrastination, and doubt before taking action. This will guarantee that we will never achieve our dreams. So, dig deep, harness your power, and take aligned action towards your goals.

69

4. Speak up

When something 'feels' wrong, it normally is. It's sometimes tough to break out of the 'good girl' stereotype and face conflict head on by speaking up if something feels wrong. As a people pleaser who likes to be liked, I just want everyone to be happy and get along. Speaking up, disagreeing, any sort of potential debate or argument can be really scary and icky. But by letting things go, allowing poor behaviour, cruel comments, rudeness, casual racism or misogyny to go unchecked, we are part of the problem. *"Silence in the face of evil is itself evil,"* Bonhoeffer. As awakened leaders, it is our responsibility to say, "this is not Okay". Use that inner strength and rise up against wrong.

5. Splat those demons!

Alongside my inner Lemon, I have gremlins. Most of us do, right? I know these demons are in my mind, and yet I feel them physically.

I have a nasty gremlin that sits in my stomach – a little voice that tells me I'm fat, stupid, useless. I've had that one for as long as I can remember. And I now also have a grief gremlin over my heart. This one says you are *too much* and *not enough* and those you love will *leave*. And yet as I grow, I'm beginning to wake up and realise it's the demons that are the useless ones and I'm soooooooo bored of them. Wasting valuable brain power on their negativity diminishes my joy, stifles my creativity and makes me miserable. I now realise that I have a responsibility to myself, my daughter and as a businesswoman to harness that Lemon positivity and splat them. So, my advice is splat those demons! Give them names if you want – really dull, boring names or evil names if you prefer – and splat them away like a nasty wasp at your summer picnic and get on with what you are here to do.

6. Use your fire for good

Don't waste too much time on being angry. Convert the fire into good energy. This is something I constantly remind myself to do and will probably resonate with divorcees navigating the complexities and challenges of 'co-parenting' (or not as the case may be!). Feelings can be a force for good but if the annoyances, the unfairness, and the hurt seep into your soul, then you can end up as a very bitter Lemon indeed. I love Michelle Obama's quote *"When they go low, we go high"* and the more awakened version of myself tries to live like this.

7. Bring your whole self to work

This may be an unpopular opinion, but my view is: bring your whole, fully authentic self to work. Work hard, bring your brilliant ideas, listen, learn, support your colleagues, laugh loudly, tell others when you're sick, cry if you need to, commiserate, and celebrate. We are human beings, not robots.

8. Accept your limitations

It's just not possible to 'have it all' all the time. In fact, it's a win if you have some of it, some of the time! Hormones, illness, life events, can all cause chaos. When I'm not at my best, rather than masking or 'soldiering on', I've learned it's better to be honest and ask for help. Accept your limitations - You don't have to be 'all the things to all the people all the time' to be loved.

9. Grab fun with both hands!

I want my epitaph to read: "She had fun". Yes, I work very, very hard, but I proactively seek opportunities for joy, for fun, for cringe, and for silliness. If there is a helter-skelter, you bet I'm sliding down it. In business and in life, there is far too much seriousness. I have proven that seriousness is not essential for success. Work makes up so much of our life and it should be fun *and* fulfilling.

10. Stay awake

Letting yourself sleepwalk in an unhappy job, home, or relationship won't deliver your goals. Wake yourself up, take action and your dreams will follow.

∼

So, mine is hardly a story straight from Disney. Let's face it, Princess and the Hysterectomy, Beauty and the Adulterous Beast – those titles don't really have a good ring to them. But I've realised nobody has a perfect life – *that* is the fairytale!

The shock of divorce and suddenly being a single mum to my 11-year-old daughter shook me awake. I've harnessed my Lemon power to build back up from ground zero into the person, woman and leader that I want to be. I'm accepting my limitations, loving myself more and I'm listening to my intuition – my inner Lemon – and I'm using this power to guide me towards a new happier, zestier and more fruitful life! I fully recommend it!

ABOUT THE AUTHOR
JENNIFER LEMON

Jennifer Lemon, Managing Partner of Customeric Consulting LLP, is a business development and bidding specialist who works with organisations of any size and any sector to help them to identify new markets and growth opportunities by helping them to write and win bids.

Through her open, collaborative, and engaging style, she builds successful relationships with clients – understanding what makes their business tick, how they're different, and how they'll meet the customer's needs. She then provides the tailored support to wrap all of this into a compelling, customer-centric winning bid.

Jennifer is trained in both PRINCE 2 and APMP and has just developed the first Ofqual accredited Level 2 and Level 3 training qualifications in Bid Fundamentals.

Jennifer lives in Stotfold, U.K. in an old Coach House near to the

River Ivel and Stotfold's ancient Watermill. She lives with her partner, daughter, and two 'Coach House Kitties', Ivel and Randall!

- Contact her to learn more about how she wins bids, via LinkedIn: Jennifer Lemon | LinkedIn or the Customeric Consulting website: https://www. customericconsulting.com/

7

METTĀ LEADERSHIP

A RESEARCHER'S TRANSFORMATIVE
DISCOVERY OF LEADING WITH LOVE
BEYOND EGO

ROBIN MILES

I needed a spark of *hope*.
I was seeking *self-understanding*.
I wanted to inspire a *shift* in the practice of leadership.

This was the longing of my soul that inspired me to research the intersection of love, mindfulness, balancing ego, and leadership, and design a practical approach to supporting leaders with cultivating an inner capacity to lead with a more formidable love ethic. But before diving in too quickly, let me briefly share the origins and influences of my transformative journey.

For as long as I can remember, leadership has been an integral part of my consciousness. As a product of the late 60's and the youngest of five children, my personal leadership ideologies were influenced and shaped by working class parents who, along with over 6 million African Americans, participated in the Great Migration from rural Southern states to the West in search of a more promising future. I idealized and relished in the presence of my older siblings, particularly my oldest sister who unapologetically embraced the edicts synonymous with the Black Power Movement – pride, self-determination, intelligence and style. Principles of high humility, integrity, respect and wielding your position, power, and influence for the greater good of others were consistently role modeled and rewarded, especially when it required having the courage to challenge the status quo, and not follow the crowd.

The first and most pivotal memory I recall being exposed to the shadow side of authority figures occurred at a grocery store during a summer vacation while visiting family in my father's hometown in Louisiana. It was an older country store with only one door for entry and exit, and as we approached, with my hand tightly held by my father's, a police officer wearing a wide-brimmed cowboy hat appeared in the doorway. Immediately, I felt an electric current flow from my father's hand to mine signaling me to behave myself, his walking pace slowed, and his entire demeanor transfigured into someone who was sullen, small, and deferential. I looked up at my father curious to understand the sudden change and hardly recognized him as the confident father that I knew him to be. Before entering the store, my father cordially greeted the officer with a slightly lowered gaze, but the same strong voice I was familiar with and relieved to hear, to which the officer responded by tipping his hat and going on about his way.

Although I may have only been about five or six years old at the time, I can still see my father's face, hear the small bell ring on the grocery store door as it opened and closed, and feel the energy transfer from my father's hand to mine like it was yesterday. I later came to understand that there were likely more complex intercultural dynamics at play in that momentary encounter than I could ever understand at that young age. However, I often recalled that formative experience throughout the decades of my human resources career as I encountered many versions of how leadership, followership, power, authority, and inequity were embodied, leveraged and, at times, irresponsibly handled.

In stark contrast to the morally virtuous principles I was nurtured in, during my corporate journey I witnessed perplexing representations of non-exemplary leadership that conflicted with my well ingrained familial values. Experiencing cognitive dissonance forced me to confront my own naivety and reflect on the attitudes, beliefs, values, and practices that the corporate environment demanded from its employees to succeed and fit in. It made me realize the importance of being aware of one's own values and principles, and finding a workplace that aligns with them. It was a difficult road for many years and conscious choices to not "play the game" or "follow the script" took a significant toll on my professional and psychological wellbeing. Nevertheless, as do many women and people of color, I persisted and forged a respectable career that spans over 25 years in leadership and organizational development. Ultimately, I came to learn that many "leaders who lose their way are not necessarily bad people; rather, they lose their moral bearings, often yielding to seductions in their paths" (George, 2011).

During a season of my life and career where I craved a challenge that would stretch me beyond my intellectual, spiritual, and professional edges, my attention shifted towards returning to graduate school. I did not begin my academic pursuits with aspirations beyond a two-year master's degree. However, after learning more about the process, I came to understand that conducting a doctoral study would allow me to apply my instinctive talent for research to make an original contribution to a field of study that I am most passionate about, transformative leadership. Narrowing down a plethora of possibilities to a meaningful area of study "rich in implications for our understanding of human nature and the nature of the world" and contributive not only to my personal transformation but also the transformation of the leaders I aspired to engage with was a more enduring process than I originally anticipated (Anderson & Braud, 2011, p. 74).

Conventionally, researchers approach identifying and selecting suitable research subjects from an approved list supplied by their institution that also align with their scholarly interests and aspirations to be published and respected as an expert in their field. My burning topic did not come to me so easily. Upon deep meditation and personal reflection, I came to realize that my proximity as a consultant to organizational leadership experiences was far too distant to intuit, understand, and articulate an industry-relevant topic that also had heart, meaning and transformative potentiality. Intuitive nudges such as these "often feel palpable as distinct perceptions into the nature of things, even as these perceptions vanish into the background of awareness when the focused, rational mind kicks in, searching for meaning" (p. 19).

Motivated by this newfound awareness, I paused my executive coaching and leadership development consultancy to reenter the corporate workforce as a global learning and development leader with hopes that a more intimate view of the lived experiences and practical development needs for organizational leaders would evoke a clearer pathway forward in my research journey. I jumped feet first into the fast-paced grind of a dynamic high-tech firm with curious eyes and an open heart. In the ensuing months, each observation, conversation, exploration of contemporary evidence-based leadership and organizational development practices, dilemma, inter- and intra-team conflict and strategic solution seemed to offer valuable breadcrumbs of perceptive insight about the lived experiences and relevant growth areas of corporate leaders.

Two years into my corporate sector re-entry, the entire world was tilted on its axis overnight by the COVID-19 global health crisis. Tangentially, another phenomenon unfolding before the world's eyes was the most epic leadership crucible of the 21st century. The word "crucible" is a derivative of the medieval Latin word *crucibulum* or vessel that alchemists used for melting metals. In modern day, we define crucibles of leadership as intense, unanticipated, and oftentimes traumatic experiences that fundamentally transforms a leader's sense of identity, depth of character, worldview, and their relationships, for better or worse. When this cataclysmic health pandemic upended the world, the institution of leadership, both subjectively and inter-subjectively, was thrusted into the global spotlight.

The weight of responsibility for the lives of others as well as themselves became a profound test that compelled many leaders to deeply self-examine and re-evaluate their values, depth of character, what really matters to them, and the legacy that they intended to leave behind. It soon became apparent that the leaders where I worked were struggling emotionally, physically, and psychologically with embracing and embodying greater levels of humanity. It was not lost on me that the expectation of abruptly switching off the "this is not personal, it is just business" ethic and switching on being more vulnerable, compassionate, empathetic, and genuinely curious about the wellbeing of employees and their families all while prioritizing self-care was much easier said than done.

Even though leaders in my organization were intellectually adept at understanding *why* these humanistic characteristics were situationally most appropriate and effectual, many did not know *how* to actually make the existential behavioral shift from being an ego-centered to human-centered leader. Interestingly, horizontal development methods that organizations traditionally use to help leaders build technical skills proved to be insufficient for this crisis. Instead, cultivating fundamental human-centered mindsets and behaviors requires leaders to vertically deepen their inner capacity to feel, think, and act with higher levels of self, systemic, and interdependent awareness. In the years leading up to the pandemic, leadership and organizational development scholars and futurists provided ample research supporting the use of interventions that prepare leaders and businesses to best respond to the increasingly unpredictable waves of complex, uncertain, and chaotic events.

Despite the forewarning evidence, vertical development interventions are still less common in organizational settings primarily because substantive growth takes considerably more time than with traditional skill building approaches. Vertical growth is a longer-term, continuous process accelerated by experiences that challenge leaders to proactively take developmental risks and actively engage with diverse perspectives to broaden their worldview and transform their sensemaking, values, and identity (Petrie, 2014). By all accounts, these observations served as breadcrumbs that began to inform the focus of my impending research study.

A generally held understanding among organizational

psychologists and sociologists is that workplace cultures are mere microcosms of the larger society. As such, the pandemic hurled the world into blending work, school and family which compounded emotional, physical, and psychological stressors in newfangled ways. This presented an unforeseeable challenge, particularly for global organizations, to support leaders in building and reinforcing their capability to help fully remote teams navigate through this impending uncertainty while staying productive and simultaneously caring for their personal and familial wellbeing. The world as we once knew it was shifting and leadership effectiveness was no longer solely being measured by productivity and profitability. The new normal required leaders to possess qualities such as flexibility, compassion, empathy, and a focus on wellbeing to build strong, resilient teams and foster a positive work culture.

As a result, developing and engaging leaders in learning experiences that cultivate these essential human-centric capabilities became one of my top priorities. During this time, due to social distancing mandates, the very same electronic and virtual technologies that were once deemed responsible for creating chasms of relational disconnect became the *only* means to communicate and stay interconnected with others. In addition to functioning as a virtual gathering platform, social media began to serve another critical role as the primary source of information, and for some, truth. The unsavory side of social media magnified as reports of the intentions of various news outlets, social interest groups and prominent, influential leaders to use the medium for self-serving, antisocial reasons became more widely known. Conversely, the concept of interbeing began to pro-socially manifest in the form of hashtag sentiments such as:

#weareallinthistogether
#StayHomeStaySafe
#QuarantineandChill
#MyPandemicSurvivalPlan
SocialDistancing
FlattenTheCurve
TogetherAtHome, etc. which electronically make it easier for

target audiences to find, share, engage and follow relevant content (Stewart, 2020; Lacsa, 2021).

Absorbing the discomfort of isolation, political polarization, racial reckoning, and overall cultural unrest and grief through a researcher's lens, I began to perceive that the universal lesson emerging through the malaise was about renewing the importance of highly valuing a fundamental love ethic and character in culture. Buzzing curiosities led to months of engaging with scholarly literature, evidence-based research, and mainstream thought leadership to finally conceive of the Mettā Leadership Study. This research endeavor was a manifestation of my desire to explore the presence, cultivation, and embodiment of love, not just as an emotion, but as a fundamental character virtue in the leadership construct of executive business leaders.

"Mettā" in Pali, the primary language of Buddhist text, is rooted in the words "gentle" and "friend," which translates in English as loving-kindness. My study distinctively defines love as a character strength that can be broadened and built with mindful intention, in contrast to well-ingrained, socially constructed and romanticized notions of love. It is the degree to which a leader values close relationships, builds that closeness in a genuine way, and understands, as well as practices self-love, extending love, and the willingness to accept love from others (Niemiec, 2014). Albeit provocative, I firmly held that investigating a practical approach for cultivating love as a core leadership competency would make for a novel contribution to the field of knowledge and leadership development scholarship and practice. I also felt that the timing, given the turbulent living and working conditions, was divinely appointed and ripe for a transformative intervention.

The key questions that guided me in this inquiry were: How might participating in a 21-day love-centered embodiment practice impact how leaders understand, relate to, and integrate love in their leadership? What common and unique experiences did they encounter on their respective journeys? How did engaging in contemplative practices inform and/or transform their leadership? The methodological approach to conducting this research is grounded in transpersonalism, a psychological construct that explores the vast expansiveness of human potential beyond the usual limits of ego (Braud & Anderson, 1998). In the study of transpersonal phenomena, "inner-experience data are essential" and presents a "more complete model for investigating human experience" (Anderson & Braud, 2011, p. 3). With the support of an amazing professional network, I recruited a multicultural and multi-gendered pool of executives from a range of small for-profit start-ups to large Fortune 100 organizations who were required to have a minimum of five years of experience at a senior director or above level and currently managing a team of at least two direct reports. In this first step, participants completed the VIA (Values in Action) Institute of Character survey and a profile results debrief to develop a baseline understanding of the underpinning research and science of character strengths, how love is characterized in this framework, and their unique personification of the framework's 24 character strengths. In the next step, participants embarked on a three-week self-directed learning experience consisting of daily intention setting, loving-kindness meditation, and self-reflective journaling to capture thoughts, emotions, and behaviors the practice evoked in the flow of their workday.

Combining mindfulness practices with character strengths development is a research-based approach aimed at activating metacognition and sustained awareness of moment-to-moment thoughts, emotions, and behaviors. Deep reflection and introspection can have a profound impact on our relationship with our mind, body, and emotions, which supports leading with greater clarity, self-awareness. Engaging in conversations with each leader about their experiences, reflections and insights was the most transformative part of the research process for me. I was absolutely blown away by how committed and courageous these leaders were to fully immerse themselves in the daily embodiment practices! It was truly inspiring to witness their dedication and discipline, and the positive impact cultivating a stronger love ethic had on their leadership and personal growth was simply amazing.

As I carefully considered and analyzed the compelling narratives shared by the participants, a compelling transformative journey began to take shape. This journey encapsulated the following love-informed shifts that the leaders navigated during their involvement in the study:

• **Befriending Oneself** – By engaging in a regular practice of sitting gracefully and self-compassionately alone with their thoughts, emotions, and feelings, leaders cultivated a well-grounded inner connection, sense of self-worth, and self-love.

• **Befriending Others** – Building a foundation of healthy self-love supported leaders with being more open and vulnerable to receiving warmth and care from others and creating shared values and conditions that normalize embodying love traits and behaviors that foster healthy interpersonal relationships, collaboration, and overall teamwork.

• **Genuine Belonging** – Cultivating, practicing, and role-modeling love-informed virtues informed new ways of thinking, relating and leading that contributed to fostering team cultures that value love character strengths and creating psychologically safe conditions amenable to team members practicing believing in themselves, taking interpersonal risks, and demonstrating genuine warmth and care towards each other.

• **Balancing and Regulating Ego** – Becoming more familiar with themselves through practicing mindful self-reflection and inquiry, leaders developed a stronger capacity to recognize and self-regulate emotional impulses, decenter personal motives, and balance the prioritization of their needs with the needs of their team members and the organization.

· · ·

• **The Alchemy of Becoming** – When leaders consistently practiced Mettā Leadership principles, they began to detach from rigid habits, recognize love character traits within themselves and others, and proactively practice new ways to action love in the daily flow of leadership.

• **Being Holistically Integrated** – At this stage of development, leaders proactively and curiously experimented with integrating newly formed conceptual insights, self-reflections, and experiences with love character-centered behaviors and mindsets.

• **Leading with Love Beyond Ego** – Leaders entered this realm when they embodied and applied love ethics and ego-awareness to new and increasingly complex situations with sustained clear intention and agency.

As a result of engaging in this study, leaders mindfully cultivated and integrated love-informed habits – self-love, gracious receptivity to love from others, and authentic befriending, warmth and care towards others – into their day-to-day leadership. Although it may be provocative and antithetical to tradition, I truly believe that the radical embracement of love character virtues is a positive step towards restoring a sense of respect and nobility in the discipline and practice of leadership.

My research journey inspired me to embrace a newfound optimism for the future state of leadership and the future state of collective harmony and prosperity throughout the world. I am confident that this current crisis of leadership is one of the world's most vital problems that must be expeditiously addressed, and leading with unwaveringly strong love character is a force longing to advance to the forefront as a principal competency imperative for all

21st century leaders. Taleb (2012) challenges that in order to survive these unprecedented times of polycrisis we must be antifragile, which is to not only resist the shocks of unforeseen turbulence, but to be resilient and use them to get better. Metaphorically, antifragility is likened to loving the wind because it is the element that energizes fire. Likewise, engaging in the deep work of building one's love character is not suited for leaders who are fragile in any way. It is a path that requires us to fully embrace antifragilism by daring to courageously withstand the shocks of this love journey, learn from it and use it to propel us forward. I extend an open invitation for all leaders and followers to join me on this Mettā Leadership path, and may Gibran's (1969) words of wisdom be a beacon light on our journey:

> And what is it to work with love?
> It is to weave the cloth with threads drawn from your heart,
> even as if your beloved were to wear that cloth.
> It is to build a house with affection,
> even as if your beloved were to dwell in that house.
> It is to sow seeds with tenderness and reap the harvest with joy,
> even as if your beloved were to eat the fruit.
> And he alone is great who turns the voice of the wind
> into a song made sweeter by his own loving.
> Work is love made visible.
> And if you cannot work with love but only with distaste,
> it is better that you should leave your work
> and sit at the gate of the temple
> and take alms of those who work with joy.

References

Anderson, R., & Braud, W. (2011). *Transforming self and others through research: Transpersonal research methods and skills for the human sciences and humanities.* Albany: State University of New York Press.

Anderson, R., & Braud, W. (2011). *Transforming self and others through research: Transpersonal research methods and skills for the human sciences and humanities.* Albany: State University of New York Press.

Braud, W., & Anderson, R. (1998). *Transpersonal research methods for the social sciences: Honoring human experience.* Thousand Oaks: Sage Publications, Inc.

D'Auria, G., & De Smet, A. (2020, March 16). *Leadership in a crisis: Responding to the coronavirus outbreak and future challenges.* Retrieved from McKinsey: https://www.mckinsey.com/business-functions/people-and-organizational-performance/our-insights/leadership-in-a-crisis-responding-to-the-coronavirus-outbreak-and-future-challenges

George, B. (2011, June 6). *Why Leaders Lose Their Way.* Retrieved 18 2017, March, from HBS Working Knowledge: Business Research for Business Leaders: http://hbswk.hbs.edu/item/why-leaders-lose-their-way

Gibran, K. (1969). *The prophet.* Alfred A. Knopf.

Hougaard, R., Carter, J., & Hobson, N. (2020, December 4). *Compassionate leadership is necessary - but not sufficient.* Retrieved from Harvard Business Publishing Corporate Learning: https://www.harvardbusiness.org/leading-through-a-pandemic/

Kerrissey, M. J., & Edmonson, A. C. (2020, April 13). *What good leadership looks like during this pandemic.* Retrieved from Harvard Business Review: https://hbr.org/2020/04/what-good-leadership-looks-like-during-this-pandemic

Lacsa, J. E. (2021). #COVID19: Hashtags and the power of social media. *Journal of Public Health*, 1-2.

Niemiec, R. M. (2014). *Mindfulness and character strengths: A practical guide to flourishing.* Boston: Hogrefe Publishing.

Petrie, N. (2014). *Vertical Leadership Development - Part 1: Developing Leaders for a Complex World.* Retrieved from Center for Creative Leadership: https://www.ccl.org/wp-content/uploads/2015/04/VerticalLeadersPart1.pdf

Silva, P., Tavares, A. F., Silva, T., & Lameiras, M. (2019). The good, the bad and the ugly: Three faces of social media used by local governments. *Government Information Quarterly, 36*, 469-479.

Stawicki, S. P., Firstenberg, M. S., & Papadimos, T. J. (2020). The growing role of social media in international health security: The good, the bad, and the ugly. *Global Health Security*, 341-357.

Stewart, A. (2020, April 6). *What's trending during coronavirus pandemic? A definitive guide to the most used hashtags.* Retrieved from The National: https://www.thenationalnews.com/arts-culture/what-s-trending-during-coronavirus-pandemic-a-definitive-guide-to-the-most-used-hashtags-1.996208

Taleb, N. N. (2012). *Antifragile: Things that gain from disorder.* New York: Random House.

86

ABOUT THE AUTHOR
ROBIN MILES

Robin Miles is an executive leadership coach and organizational development consultant with over 25 years of HR leadership experience. She has a versatile background building and executing global programs "from the ground up" in the areas of Organizational Change, Leadership Development, Team Effectiveness, Employee Relations and Diversity, Equity & Inclusion.

Robin is currently a Ph.D. candidate in the Transformative Studies graduate program at the California Institute of Integral Studies. Her qualitative research examines the use of contemplative practices designed to engage business executives in an embodied orientation, cultivation, and integration of non-egoic, love-centered virtues in their day-to-day leadership. Robin is a California Bay Area native and in her leisure enjoys traveling, taking scenic coastal drives, and making memories with friends and family.

- If you are inspired to learn more about how you and/or your team can experience a transformative Mettā

Leadership® journey, please submit an inquiry on her website at rmiles@mettaleadershipenterprises.org to receive a free 30-minute consultation.

8

INVISIBLE LEADERSHIP

DR JOY HESS

Weeding

I love flowers - their colors, petals, and beautiful, varied fragrances. I wish I had a garden, but I hate weeding. I suppose I could learn to love it, but I live in Florida and the sun gets really, really hot. So, who would have thought that weeding would change my life?

It was 2020, I was an empty-nester, single mom, trying to find my place without my kids. The previous 12 months had been rough. While the world was in pandemic mode, I was putting my life back together. 2019 started with the death of my mom after a long battle with dementia, I was her primary caregiver. A few months later, my father moved across the country from Illinois to Florida, his duty to my mom completed. He had his own dreams to chase, even at 84. A few months later, a dear friend and mentor also moved across the country. She was someone who always made me feel safe and protected, now I was on my own. Then another close friend, peer and mentor passed away from addiction, much too young. And then another. Then the hospital I worked at (and loved dearly) closed. It was a busy year for me, in my world COVID was practically non-existent (except when I was sick with it), I was so caught up in my own losses.

Professionally, I was learning more and more about trauma informed care in the neonatal intensive care unit (NICU) and took a course with Mary Coughlin with *Caring Essentials*. The course introduced me to Mel MacIntyre, a life coach. A single, private session with her was part of the course. I already knew I didn't need or want a life coach. Yes, I had had a tough year, but I had direction, faith, and a good support system. Yet somehow, during our call, I found myself intrigued by her ideas and the things she asked me to consider about my life. I decided to take a full course with her called *Becoming Wildly Authentic*. It was in this course I learned about weeding.

Mel asked me to call to mind the negative beliefs I held about myself and to investigate where they came from. Seemed easy enough. I searched my mind for proof of why I wasn't smart enough, thin enough, successful enough and lastly, why I was a second-rate neonatal nurse practitioner. One by one, I realized these were stories I told myself, believed wholeheartedly yet there was no real evidence of their truth. I looked at each of those beliefs and pulled them out by the roots. I weeded the garden of my mind.

From that day forward, it was all very simple. I simply didn't include those negative thoughts as part of my identity. Almost like magic, I performed medical procedures better, I felt better about myself and started treating my body better, I settled into my accomplishments, reflected on my life, and realized I was just simply satisfied. Happy. Just like that.

What does this have to do with leadership? My position as a nurse practitioner is inherently one of leadership - teaching nurses, mentoring other nurse practitioners (NPs) and leading in the care of my patients. Not until I did the weeding, did I embrace these aspects of leadership. Once I embraced them, it felt so easy, so natural, so humbling, so satisfying. Like putting on my favorite jeans. My leadership took the form of words of encouragement, a few extra minutes to sit and listen, taking time to explain why I made the clinical decision I made, staying calm in the middle of chaos and setting the tone for the team. Sometimes, it was just taking time to consider the people around me, and what their experiences were. I found that so many people just need that, and it's so simple. They lack confidence in themselves (as I did) and with a little encouragement, they are able to take a step on their own in confidence.

This catapulted me to my next level of leadership. The way I cared for my body.

No sugar, no flour

Drastic, right? Well, so is amputation or blindness from unrelenting diabetes. I don't have diabetes, thank God, but I sure didn't want to get it! I struggled with my weight all my life, but especially since I became a nurse practitioner (my new colleagues and I liked to order out quite frequently). Downtown Chicago offered an endless buffet of amazing choices. Fast forward to 2020, once my life started to slow down, after my mom was gone, my dad had moved and kids were trying their wings, I took the time to really evaluate what I had done with my life up to that point. Some things I was very happy with, some not so much. My body and how I had treated it was in the "not so much" category. My weight had always held me back from the activities I really wanted to do and now I was at my heaviest.

I have always loved the water, especially the ocean, but I don't love bathing suits. I had clothes in my closet in a myriad of sizes, I fit into a minority of them. I decided it was time to climb this mountain. I started a comprehensive eating program of no sugar and no flour, (this is due to the addictive properties of them both), bound quantities and no snacking. Once I had eliminated sugar and flour, went through sugar detox, and was eating protein, vegetables, fruits and whole grains, something amazing happened. My mind cleared, my cravings disappeared, the mental chatter over food disappeared and I was able to "show up" in my life in a way I hadn't known possible. Oh, and I lost a significant amount of weight as a nice bonus. Instead of living my life around what I may or may not eat, I ate around the way I lived my life.

Once I was able to treat my body better by what I fueled it with, I was also able to sleep better and I had more room for things like reading, sitting quietly and prayer. Years ago, I took a "train the trainer" course to teach at a nurse assistant training program. One morning, the instructor showed up five minutes late, her papers flying, pens falling on the floor, keys dropping- she was totally flustered as the class waiting in the hall watched. Once we were all settled inside the classroom, she told us that it was all an act-she was showing us how *not* to show up to teach a class. She made her point. Over the years, that had become my life's M.O., flying by the seat of my pants, running late, slightly disorganized. After that strong impression she made, I tried to pull myself together in that respect, but it wasn't until I got my eating habits under control that I realized how important it is to take the time to be early, be prepared and show up with calm confidence. This is a crucial part of leadership. You are the backbone, the safety net, the bowling bumpers, the wise one. Not the arrogant one, not the bossy one, not the micromanager one. It's not about you, it's never about you, it's about those you mentor. It was about you before, but now you step aside and let others grow with the warmth of your sun, not freeze in your shadow.

I had to achieve a place of symbiosis with my body and my health, and then my mind before I could gently step aside and quietly show others how to grow in their goals and dreams.

Oh, and remember how I love the ocean? Once my body (and mind) felt better I learned to S.C.U.B.A. dive, just before I turned 50. I didn't do it earlier because my garden hadn't been properly weeded yet. I thought someone my size could never dive (totally untrue), admittedly, it was easier minus a few pounds. I continued to dive two to three times a month for two years. Those were some of my happiest memories. What does SCUBA diving have anything to do with leadership? The best way to teach or guide is by example. I wanted to do something, so I did.

However, 2022 brought new changes. I let go of my good eating habits, gained the weight back and was so desperately unhappy with my body again. It took me until just this year to get a handle on it, I'm back to my good habits and all the other good that comes with it.

Heading south

In 2021 I was in Illinois and I had two jobs I loved. I lived in an old townhouse converted from a coat factory built in the 1800's (the kind with exposed brick, mechanicals and 17 foot ceilings). I was financially secure, I had just started working on my doctorate degree, when I realized that my father could no longer live alone down in Fort Myers. This is the dilemma that so many people my age must face, how to care for aging parents. At that time my dad was 86 and he had been in and out of the hospital for several months. I had been traveling back and forth between Chicago and Florida all through COVID to help him. Did I mention I am an only child?

My options were to hire a caregiver, have him go to assisted living or take care of him myself. Options A and B were not palatable for me. He is, after all, my father. I took care of my mom at home for many years, so why not him? Even so, this was a tough decision since I was in such a happy place in my life. So, I prayed. I really prayed. I asked God to guide me and show me the next right thing to do. I resigned to not knowing how the whole plan would turn out, I only needed the next step. I trusted that God would figure out the rest. I trusted Him with my whole heart and soul.

I had been on a retreat the year before to St. Augustine, Florida. That was one of those experiences that had a profound impact on my life. Fast forward to 2021, and I felt I should reach out to the director of that retreat for his advice. He is a public figure, but somehow, I found his (nearly) private email. Not expecting a response, I described my situation and asked his advice. To my surprise he responded within five minutes. This was the gist of his response:

"Whatever you do, when you put the Lord first and want his will, he will bless you. Even if you pick what might be second best, I'll turn it into the first best because of your attitude and your love of Him." He went on "But just remember, Matthew 6:33 "Seeking first the kingdom of God and his righteousness and all the other things will be added to you." Put Jesus and his church first, and he'll bless whatever decision you make. Of this I am certain!" I read his response several times with tears in my eyes. I felt God was speaking directly to me.

I took this to heart and put my beloved townhome up for sale, I interviewed all over Florida, and found a job with enough flexibility for me to care for my dad at home. I turned in resignations and said goodbye to all I had ever known. I bought a home in Zephyrhills, FL sight unseen. I moved in July 2022. I moved my dad up with me in August 2022. On Sept 27, 2022, Hurricane Ian destroyed Fort Myers. My dad had been living in a high rise apartment building right on the canal-directly in Ian's path. In our new home, we were completely untouched. "Seeking first the kingdom of God and his righteousness and all the other things will be added to you." I just wanted the next step. God has never let me down. I know He wants me to be my best self, I must simply ask for his guidance and then wait and listen. This is where silence and prayer come in. God speaks in the silence of the heart. He doesn't compete with Netflix or TikTok.

My Florida adventure got even better. My job turned out better than I could have ever imagined, I have met some amazing friends down here. I completed my Doctor of Nursing Practice (DNP) and best of all, I am spending time with my dad. What good is a life if you can't give it away in service? That is leadership.

Humility

Not my forte. Pride fits me much better, much easier. A little lonelier, but effective.

Or was it?

When I look back at how pride has served me in my life. Like the time I yelled at the old man snow blowing his drive, but went a little too far into the street at the exact moment when my car slid a bit of ice. A minor accident, obviously "his fault" (no injuries). Or when as a young adult I called my dad an a** h*** because he accidentally hit my car pulling out of the drive, only for me to realize the neighbors were watching. Those are the moments I would pay any price to rewrite. I was met, in both people I had hurt, with wisdom I didn't yet possess. They let me rant and rave and simply apologized. Is this why

I am now able to respond with calm patience and kindness to others who treat me pridefully?

Humility is a funny thing. To muster it, I almost have to physically pause, take a breath, lower my tense shoulders, and start with "you're right", let's look at it from your point of view. This has a nearly 100% success rate in disarming someone who is picking a fight. And honestly, who wants to fight? I'm closer to the end than the beginning of my life, and I want to spend my days happy, fulfilled, learning, and in service, not fighting.

Humility is not synonymous with passivity or cowardice. Quite the opposite. There is a magical point where the right amount of humility and confidence intersect, and I find that is one of the most attractive qualities in a human being. When pride is set aside, then connection and communication really flourish.

Humility is the most important quality of a leader. Without it, everything becomes about you. With it, you can take a step back and, in service, give others the tools they need to succeed (because your ego doesn't need the credit). As a leader, your goal is to help others with theirs. It's not about you. It's about them. Comparing a situation to a stage play, the best leaders are off stage left, behind the curtains, making sure the set is in order, the costumes are on, the lines are memorized, the orchestra is in tune and the spotlight is on someone else. The leader's name isn't even in the program.

Confidence

Where does confidence come from? The National Institute of Health describes it this way "Confidence comes from feelings of well-being, acceptance of your body and mind and belief in your own ability, skills and experience." OK, but what happens if you don't have ability or skills or experience? How does a child gain confidence? Should confidence be dependent on something that can be temporary (ability or skill)? Why not base it on core beliefs in who you are at the depth of your soul? If you can't do that, then maybe it's time to look at the deepest part of your soul and make some changes.

My first course in my doctoral program was a leadership course.

As part of the final project, we did a personality assessment and wrote about what kind of leaders we are. That took some adjusting. I thought she meant what kind of leader I would become. I was wrong. As I digested that reality, I completed the Meyers Briggs Personality test. I am an INFJ-A (intuitive, feeling, judging, assertive – advocate). My role is diplomat, and my strategy is confident individualism. Doing this project felt like permission to be exactly who I am, believe in what I hold true deep in my soul and lead from there. No changes, no compromise, just be me. Maybe I'm not a traditional leader, but I am a unique leader. The world already has plenty of traditional leaders, but they didn't have me. At least then. Now they do.

"For it was you who formed my inward parts; you knit me together in my mother's womb. I praise you, for I am fearfully and wonderfully made"

— PSALM 139: 14-15

I am grateful to be unique. I am grateful that I can be authentically myself. I strive daily to find that beautiful balance between humility and confidence.

Authentic transparency

This is something I didn't understand until I experienced it. I thought everyone had a side they hid from the world and a "public" side. Trust me, that is exhausting. Being authentic is much easier. Why have a side that you have to hide, why not just make that side "better"? Become a person you aren't ashamed of on the outside *or* on the inside. There was an old novel from the 1980s about a woman who moved to Beverly Hills to find success and then revenge. Although I don't recommend the revenge part, she touched many lives in the meantime. One was a struggling actor, trying to reinvent himself in a Paul Newman kind of way. Her advice to him was "the world already has Paul Newman, but the world doesn't have Roy

Lombardo". In other words, be unapologetically yourself. God made us each unique-our looks, personalities, our weaknesses, and our gifts. These were given to us for a very specific and necessary purpose. They are knit into our DNA. All we must do is say "yes" to how we are to use these unique quirks and qualities. Trust me, when the inside matches the outside it's like being set free.

Phone a friend

Why reinvent the wheel? Any successful leader knows who to turn to for advice, reassurance, consultation or just a venting session. I have collected some short words of wisdom that I use daily and I teach when appropriate. Here they are:
- Speak kindly to yourself, you are always listening (@fatgirlfedup).
- God can write straight with our crooked lines (*Life is Messy* by Matthew Kelly)
- It is only when you really believe something to be true that it motivates you to action (unknown-seen on the wall in a pizza place in Seattle)
- Pray, hope and don't worry (Saint Padre Pio)
- Emotions are always temporary
- I wish you could see yourself through my eyes (every parent, ever)
- Let it roll off your back like water off a duck's back (my dad)
And in the end, love.
"Not all of us can do great things. Do small things with great love" said Saint Mother Theresa of Calcutta. She sure gave us a good example of that. What else is there? What can you take with you at the end of your life? I recall reading a reflection from Mel, my life coach, after her father passed away. She had been his caregiver, like I am for my father. She realized that in the end, love is all that matters. No homes, or cars, shoes, degrees, vacations, or fancy dinners. Just love. No TV shows, no ego, no quarreling. Just love. And how the end can be filled with love is by loving those around you-friend or foe-in

small ways. Humble ways. Selfless ways. Be able to smile when someone else succeeds, not be secretly happy when they fail. Make the inside as beautiful as the outside. Take a step to the side, so others can bask in the warmth of the sun.

ABOUT THE AUTHOR
DR JOY HESS

Dr Joy Hess is a neonatal nurse practitioner, speaker and emerging healthcare leadership consultant. She is passionate about helping men and women develop natural leadership skills within themselves, particularly where faith and healthcare intersect. Joy has earned a Doctor of Nursing Practice from Gannon University with a focus on trauma informed care in the NICU/obstetrics. She has a passion for the care of neonates and works as a neonatal nurse practitioner, having earned her MSN and BSN from Rush University in Chicago, IL. She teaches Neonatal Resuscitation and the S.T.A.B.L.E. program, and formerly taught in the nurse assistant training program at Oakton Community College. Joy speaks and gives presentations on resilience in nursing, trauma informed care in the NICU as well as other medical topics. She is currently enrolled in a spiritual direction program at Divine Mercy University. Joy lives in Florida where she cares for her elderly father. She enjoys watching her three young adult children spread their wings and chase their dreams. She began SCUBA just three years ago and enjoys diving in the Florida Keys.

9

PROGRESSION ISN'T ALWAYS A STRAIGHT LINE

ELAINE TROUP

Many of us live in silence with our challenges, unsupported and unseen. I'm not alone in this. Like so many others, I navigated my way through each situation without sharing my deepest feelings. There isn't one single event that I can pinpoint as my turning point. More a relentless series of events that compounded and had a recurring theme, a silence. I hope this chapter encourages at least one person to talk about their situation. In my experience the world is waiting to help you.

I thought the fear I once felt over my financial security was my turning point. And in many ways, it was. Life has changed immeasurably since then and unquestionably for the better. I'm grateful for the second chance and the sense of love and belonging that I now cherish with my partner, stepdaughter, son and daughter. But it wasn't always like that.

I felt badly treated in a previous relationship, which I'm embarrassed and disappointed to admit. It's almost like it didn't happen to me. It wasn't awful, it just never felt good enough. But I had a strong network of support, no children (despite a real desire for them), and no real commitments beyond a mortgage and some debt. I also had a career in property.

Something needed to change, I was growing increasingly

uncomfortable with my financial situation. The debt was increasing, and I had a genuine fear for my own financial security. I needed to take back control and I knew that property could provide this for me.

Early days

My career in property began in an architectural practice in Glasgow but quickly my focus moved to urban design and physical regeneration projects. I understood the significance of public spaces, built environment and how the view that greets you from your window can impact both your health and perception of life chances. Regenerating physical environments was work that I believed could have a positive impact on communities and on the quality of life of many people. My passion was always property, but I was drawn to the idea of the greater good.

I was in my 20s and I was having a ball. I was committed to and loved my work, my colleagues became friends, and I bought my first flat. It was amazing, the sense of independence was wonderful. Now I had savings, a great property and things were going well. I had the odd challenge and was very aware of the male-dominated environment I was working in, but I felt confident.

Networking has always been a big part of my professional life and I remain forever grateful for the encouragement I received to make this a core part of my career. It was sound advice then and remains so now. The connections I made over 20 years continue to be a source of support to this day.

As my career progressed, I took on various committee positions within a national networking organisation, Women in Property. The aim of the organisation is to 'seek an industry that is balanced, diverse and inclusive'. (www.womeninproperty.org.uk). From member to Secretary, Vice Chair and Chair of the Central Scotland branch, I learned so many skills and built solid connections through the years. I would recommend this organisation to any woman working in the property sector.

Of course I had the time to network and to look after my health and wellbeing, but I was soon to learn that priorities change.

After a short marriage I found myself in a very different situation. That wonderfully positive feeling of being in control with money when I bought my first flat had seriously diminished. It had been a gradual process. On the one hand I was in control of my money, of course. I've always maintained my own bank accounts, and always will. But the decision on where to direct my money was influenced by mounting debts that I felt were largely not of my making. I felt I had no option; I was working to service debts. Despite how I was feeling I kept this to myself. I never shared my feelings with my friends or family, I just continued in silence.

Look at a photograph of me from that time and you might not see it. But it was there, in my heart and in my head. I was struggling but mentioned it to no one. I thought I was covering up well but the words of my mum proved otherwise when one weekend she asked me quietly 'Are you ok?'. I knew straight away what she meant. 'No, but I will be,' was my answer.

Soon after, I moved back to my parents' house, not something you think you'll ever need to do. My emotions were mixed but as I was greeted by my dad's hug he asked, 'what took you so long?', the sense of relief was incredible and I felt myself melt into his arms. I didn't need to pretend anymore. I was home and I was going to be ok.

Worrying about what people would think, and especially what pain or upset it would cause my parents was one of the biggest barriers for me. But it turns out, those that love you the most probably already know when things aren't right. If only we had their foresight!

I was 38, living with my parents, working two jobs and, thanks to no longer living a silent lie, I was once again feeling unstoppable. After what seemed like an age, I was regaining control. I started to invest in myself, buying some new clothes and looking after my health. I joined a gym and started feeling stronger and fitter. I rebuilt my social life and re-focussed on my career. By now I had moved from the private to the public sector.

And after breaking my own silence, other women started to share. Many commented on my 'bravery', on their wish to do something similar, their plans to act when the kids were older. I came to realise that so many of us are living through some of our biggest challenges in silence. I wanted to shake them and tell them to do it, take back control of their lives. But of course, we each have our unique situation and our own time for taking action and it was this realisation that, years later, would help to shape my property business.

I learned a lot about myself and others during that time and I told myself I would never lose control of my finances again. As soon as I could, just two years after moving back to my parents, I bought my own investment property. It was my safety net and the start of my next chapter.

My family

Fast forward a few years and after much heartache I was able to start my own family with my new partner. Maybe this was when I began to question my career plans. I have always wanted to have my own business but for various reasons it hadn't happened yet. I had the experience, the knowledge and while I wasn't quite there with my business idea, it was taking shape.

I gave birth to our son in early 2019 and returned to my management role in the public sector at the end of January 2020. You know what's coming next, don't you? Within only seven weeks post-maternity leave I found myself working as part of a team to establish a whole new service in an emergency response to Covid-19. Looking back at those weeks and months, I'm not quite sure how we managed. It was an immensely stressful time for everyone and the pressure of setting up a new service ensured I kept going.

I was determined that when I was home with my stepdaughter and son, I was going to be present, to be fully with them. This of course meant working evenings. Exhausting, stressful and probably all a bit much for me on my recent return to work. Did I speak out? Did I voice my feelings to the workplace? No, of course not. I was proud of my resilience, my work ethic. I was exhausted but I kept going. And the silence was creeping back.

The pandemic was a heartbreaking time for so many of us. It

threw us into a world that we didn't recognise and put us through events we could never have imagined. I had the privilege of working with a wonderful team of committed talented people providing services to the most vulnerable people in our communities. And while the challenge of designing and providing a new service brought a sense of professional pride, the stress of doing so took its toll.

On 3 April 2020 my beautiful dad died. He had suffered in silence for so many years with Ankylosing spondylitis, a debilitating illness, the treatment for which only added painful side effects. He was the heart of our family and we've never fully recovered from his passing.

While Covid-19 didn't impact on my dad's health, it had a huge impact on his final days, on me and our family. Not being allowed to travel with dad in the ambulance on his final journey. Not being allowed to stay with my mum on the night he was taken to hospital. Not being allowed, not being allowed, not being allowed! Not being allowed to hug my brother, or even have my sister attend the sparsely attended funeral was and continues to be heartbreaking.

At that point we weren't allowed inside others' houses, although we quickly created our own bubble so that Mum didn't have to be alone. But there seemed little point in taking bereavement leave given the circumstances, and the ongoing crisis we were dealing with at work. So, I continued working and dealing with whatever was thrown at me. It wasn't until the funeral three weeks later that I took any leave. In hindsight, I should have. And even now, writing this chapter I feel that I still need time to heal.

My resilience and emotional intelligence

I've always had pride in my personal resilience, of having never taken a day off work. I almost wore it as a badge of honour. But so what? Maybe it's only with years of experience that you learn that yes, a good work ethic is important but not if it has a negative impact on your wellbeing.

Throughout life we are dealt different challenges and we learn to cope with them. But all too often we do so without sharing our experiences, we keep them to ourselves. Something, maybe our upbringing, society, friends or colleagues, keeps us quiet, never sharing any perceived weakness or vulnerability. Whatever the reason behind it, the silence we shroud ourselves in is counterproductive. I've learned that by sharing our stories, experiences and journeys, we strengthen relationships and, in so doing, help ourselves and others.

I wear my heart on my sleeve, there's no denying that. But through my career I always felt this was a negative, that showing emotions especially in such a male-dominated workplace wouldn't be beneficial. And so, like many others, I learned to put on a tough outer shell, to keep the emotions and vulnerabilities away from the job.

I remember deciding to leave a job. I spoke to a senior manager at the time and couldn't avoid showing my emotions but I got nothing in return – nothing! Not long after, that same manager decided to leave the organisation and reached out to me to empathise with the emotions I'd shared previously. In that moment, we created a stronger bond. This was a lightbulb moment for me – the benefit of the emotional connection.

Today I consider my emotional intelligence to be one of my absolute strengths. And we're not talking about me being emotional, that's just me. Instead, what I've learned is that every time I've shared a bit of my own feelings or vulnerability, it strengthens a relationship. It changes something with those around me. It can be immensely powerful.

During my time in leadership roles my biggest successes have come when the relationships are strongest, when I've connected with colleagues to develop a sense of trust and understanding. Maintaining professionalism while taking time to engage individually, giving a bit of insight into my own life, I often get so much more back from others.

It can be tough; some people have a lot of pressure and worry in their life. But for me, understanding this helps me to lead teams more effectively. It builds trust and mutual respect. It allows me to be seen by others, leading them to be the best they can and deliver the best team results.

Being present, approachable and open to ideas makes the

majority of those I work alongside feel supported to generate ideas. And these are normally brilliant ideas that we can run with. A win-win situation.

Losing that sense of control again

A couple of years on from Covid and my family is complete with the birth of our daughter in 2022. A true gift. We were now a family of five and my heart was set on owning my own business.

The week that I returned to work after my second maternity leave, I attended a management meeting to discuss the pending team changes. I'd known what I was going back to. I'd been involved in some high-level phone calls during my maternity leave, but it didn't prepare me for this. It was overwhelming.

There were organisational decisions being taken in response to its financial situation and we were the early casualties. Things were changing and I had no control over what was to come.

I began doubting the decisions that had brought me here. Should I have stayed in a different sector? Should I have specialised? Doubt and a feeling of dread were overtaking me. I'd never in my career felt so low.

I felt on the brink of a breakdown, a crash, a burnout. Whatever you want to call it, juggling my family, career and health was not working for me. Was one aspect of my life suffering? No, every aspect of my life was suffering. I knew that how I was feeling wasn't sustainable. Once again, I needed to recover my sense of control and this time I needed to talk about it.

It took a lot for me to finally vocalise how I was feeling and when I did I was blessed with love, support and understanding. But the day I found myself sitting at my desk in my small garden office, with tears pouring down my face was the day I picked up the phone to a counselling service. Nothing particular had happened that morning to provoke the tears. I was just ready.

Starting my business

The pressure I was experiencing at work, together with the longing to have more flexibility in my life motivated me to start my own property business. My family, my health and a need for a greater sense of control over my future were driving me. And it was the loving support of my family and my own resilience that enabled me to start my business, working in the evenings, while remaining committed to my day job.

My expertise in property was now backed up with some valuable life experience. I knew that women remain hugely under-represented in the property industry and I was passionate about supporting positive change to increase female representation. I also knew that I had found a sense of financial security through previous property investments and that I wanted to build on this for my family and for others.

My career in property and my on-going work in some of the most deprived areas in Scotland has cemented my motivation to help women to a more sustainable financial footing, through property. Today my mission in business is to support women to invest confidently in property, whether that be to secure their own safe domestic environment, to increase their passive income or benefit from longer-term capital appreciation. From my experience, property offers so many options.

Final thoughts

Writing this chapter has been a real privilege and an emotional roller-coaster. I have gained so much from it. It's been a snippet of my journey so far that reflects my resilience, my personal growth and my approach to leadership all of which I believe has been influenced by my parents and those around me.

Each of us will face different challenges, will have different levels of support and will respond in our own unique way. Here are some of the things I've learned, I hope that they resonate with you:

Silence – so many times through my personal and professional life, I have dealt with challenges in silence. I've always needed time to 'digest' events, to mull things over. However, there is a recurring theme in that I rarely shared my feelings, my struggles with those around me and, with hindsight, how I wished I had. If you take nothing else from this chapter, please take an awareness that we all have our challenges and I invite and encourage you to talk about them! You and others will benefit from it.

Emotional intelligence – being confident to share a bit of your own vulnerability goes a long way. But true emotional intelligence isn't about opening up with everyone regardless. It's about having sufficient perception to recognise when it's appropriate and when an individual would respond better to an alternative approach.

Progression – isn't always a straight line. When I was studying architecture at university, I thought that I'd always be an architect. It never occurred to me that my career would take a different path. But it has and that's ok. My personal life took its own path and, while tough at times, I don't regret any part of it. Each step provided me with opportunities to grow and learn more about myself. It's ok to retreat for a while, ponder and then share vulnerabilities before coming back stronger and wiser.

Take control – a few times over the years I've experienced control slipping away from me. And each time I've taken action to regain control. We can't control the entire world around us, but for many of us there are aspects that we can. Taking positive action where I could, provided me with a greater sense of calm and direction. This includes starting my business in my free time while still working. Just knowing that I had done something positive was enough to regain that sense of control. Something that I need in my life.

Financial security – money is important. We all need it. Money provides for us and our loved ones. And of course, everyone will have their view of the best ways to ensure financial security. Personally, property has provided this for me and I hope that by reading this you might consider your own property investment options. I'd love to know how you get on and of course, I'd love to help you on your own journey.

ABOUT THE AUTHOR
ELAINE TROUP

Elaine Troup is the owner of Prospera Property and lives with her partner and family near Glasgow. She has a background in architecture and physical regeneration of the built environment with over 17 years in the property sector, receiving multiple awards for her work. Most recently her career has focussed on promoting individual and community resilience through empowerment. She also contributes to the ever-present challenge of tackling food insecurity.

Elaine's love for property and the security it can provide has led her to her most recent venture. With the combination of her private and public sector experience, together with some valuable life experience, she now helps people to maximise their investments through property.

- www.prosperaproperty.co.uk
- Elaine Troup | LinkedIn

ABOUT THE PUBLISHER
DINA BEHRMAN

Inspired World Publishing was founded by former journalist-turned-PR strategist and publisher, Dina Behrman.

Dina works with entrepreneurs and business leaders to help them stop being the internet's best kept secret, become the 'go to' expert and create a much bigger impact in the world by sharing their story and expertise in multi-author books and in the press.

She launched her business following a decade working as a journalist, during which she was published in virtually every national UK newspaper and many magazines. She's worked as a publicist for a number of industry leaders, and has also helped hundreds of entrepreneurs learn how to do their own PR. She's been featured in Forbes, Entrepreneur, Huff Post, The Guardian, BBC radio, amongst others. To find out more visit www.dinabehrman.com

Printed in Great Britain
by Amazon

43692492R00069